Eve ___ ___
ιο Walsingham

Elizabeth Ruth Obbard ODC was a novice mistress at the Carmel of Walsingham when she wrote *The History and Spirituality of Walsingham* and *A Walsingham Prayer Book*, inspired by her experience of welcoming pilgrims and visitors to 'England's Nazareth'. These two popular titles, now out of print, form the basis of this new book.

Sr Elizabeth is now based at The Friars in Aylesford, Kent, where she continues her work of leading retreat and pilgrimage groups.

Every Pilgrim's Guide to Walsingham

'England's Nazareth'

Elizabeth Ruth Obbard

CANTERBURY
PRESS
Norwich

First published in 2007 by The Canterbury Press Norwich (a publishing imprint of Hymns Ancient & Modern Limited, a registered charity)
9–17 St Alban's Place, London N1 0NX

www.scm-canterburypress.co.uk

British Library Cataloguing in Publication data
A catalogue record for this book is available from the British Library

ISBN 978-1-85311-808-1

Typeset by Regent Typesetting, London
Printed in the UK by CPI Bookmarque, Croydon, CR0 4TD

Contents

Contents

Maps, illustrations and photographs

Photographs on the inside front and back covers

Aerial view of Walsingham Abbey (Photo: Mike Page)
Looking into the interior of the holy house,
Anglican Shrine (Photo: Louis Quail)
Lighting candles in the Anglican Shrine holy house
(Photo: Louis Quail)
View of Slipper Chapel and RC Shrine
(Photo © Roman Catholic Shrine)

Maps, illustrations and photographs in main text

Introduction

Walsingham – A Village and its Shrines

The present-day pilgrim to Walsingham finds a village where time seems to have entered timelessness. Norfolk itself is a county of wide skies, its fields colourful with magnificent expanses of wheat, barley, flax, lavender, reaching as far as the eye can see. There are masses of red poppies and delicate displays of white Queen Anne's lace along the hedgerows, with birds and butterflies in abundance. This is the county of black-faced sheep, of church towers and spires rising from

the middle of every hamlet. There are numerous monastic ruins too – Binham, Bromholm, Castle Acre and many more, their stones telling of an age long past which still seems to linger.

Norfolk villages, now so sadly depleted, were once alive with the business of a thriving wool trade. The fields produced abundant food for everyone and the hardy sheep made Norfolk rich in wool and woven cloth, attracting medieval immigrants from the Low Countries who brought their own skills and style of building to add variety and beauty to the landscape. In those days Norwich was the second city of the realm after London, a centre of industry with a fine cathedral served by Benedictine monks, and a woman writer and mystic who would one day become one of the most famous of Norfolk's daughters, Julian of Norwich.

North Norfolk, where Walsingham is situated, is slightly more undulating than the southern part of the county. Turning down a winding road which runs through a shallow valley, the traveller passes through the village of Houghton-le-Dale with its parish church dedicated to St Giles, patron saint of cripples; and there, on the opposite side of the River Stiffkey, standing beside the twentieth-century Chapel of Reconciliation, stands the ancient Slipper Chapel, where, in pre-Reformation times, pilgrims were wont to remove their shoes before walking the last 'holy mile' into Walsingham, England's Nazareth, in their bare feet.

Procession through the streets of Walsingham

A mile further on, the present-day pilgrim reaches the village of Little Walsingham, with its narrow main street and overhanging gabled houses. Behind a large medieval gatehouse at the top of the High Street lie the ruins of the

Augustinian Priory (now termed 'the Abbey') where a solitary arch dissects the skyline. Once this was the religious establishment whose great church housed the replica of the home at Nazareth, and which boasted the precious image of Our Lady of Walsingham. Turning by the village pump one sees the Anglican Shrine Church, completed in 1938, which contains a new holy house.

The medieval town pump in the Common Place

For Walsingham's past is also a contemporary reality. Here Mary seems as much present as when the Lady Richeldis first saw to the erection of a little chapel in honour of Mary's joy at the Annunciation. In those days Walsingham rivalled Jerusalem, Rome and Compostella as a pilgrimage destination. Today it has become once more a place of pilgrimage, of peace and of healing.

This book will tell you Walsingham's story, and enable you to make your own pilgrimage of faith in union with the thousands of people who have walked these roads before you. Here Mary continues to share with those who come the secret of holiness, that of saying 'Yes' to God in our own lives, and doing so with joy and humility.

1

Practical Information for Pilgrims and Visitors

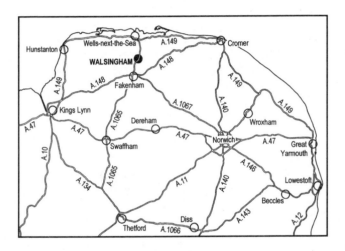

GETTING TO WALSINGHAM

By car or coach

Several roads converge at the bustling market town of Fakenham, a few miles south of Walsingham.

If approaching from the Norwich direction on the A1067, turn right at the roundabout on the outskirts of Fakenham, and keep straight on at the next roundabout. At the third roundabout, turn left onto the by-pass (A148 from Cromer, via Holt) which skirts the northern edge of the town. Follow this road for about 1½ miles, before turning right onto the B1105 signposted Wells-next-the-Sea and Walsingham.

From the south, on the A1065 from Swaffham, keep straight on at the roundabout to the west of the town (by a large petrol filling station) onto the A148 by-pass, and about 250 yards further on, turn left onto the B1105. For travellers approaching from King's Lynn on the A148, bear left at the roundabout by the filling station, and take the turning left onto the B1105.

Once on the B1105, follow this road for about 4½ miles into Walsingham. (In reality *Little* Walsingham which, despite its name, is considerably larger than its near neighbour *Great* Walsingham!) This is attractive, rolling countryside rising to over 250ft above sea-level – high for Norfolk – and about half-way between Fakenham and Walsingham the road crests a rise to give spectacular views of East Barsham Manor, a magnificent early Tudor red-brick mansion. It is believed that Henry VIII stayed here before making a pilgrimage – on foot – to Walsingham; the last in an unbroken line of 14 successive monarchs to do so.

If travelling along the A149 coast road, turn onto the B1105 on the outskirts of Wells-next-the-Sea to reach Walsingham, only 4 miles to the south.

Public transport

As with most rural areas, public transport is limited and visitors are strongly advised to check up-to-date timetables with the service operators indicated before undertaking a journey. Please remember that timetables may vary between seasons.

Bus and coach

First Eastern Counties operate bus services in much of Norfolk, with routes 56 and 56A running 4 or 5 times daily between Norwich and Fakenham.

> First Eastern Counties, Rouen House, Rouen Road, Norwich NR1 1RB Tel: 08456 020121 Fax: 01603 615438
> Website: www.firstgroup.com/ukbus/easterncounties

Sanders Coaches provide bus and coach services primarily in north-east Norfolk, including route 45 from Fakenham via Walsingham to Holt.

> Sanders Coaches Ltd, Hempstead Road, Holt, Norfolk NR25 6JU Tel: 01263 712800 Fax: 01263 710920 Email: info@sanderscoaches.com See also their website at http://sanderscoaches.com/timetables

The most extensive network in the west and north-west of the county is provided by King's Lynn based **Norfolk Green**. Route X29 runs between Norwich and Fakenham, and as route 29 continues through Walsingham to terminate at Wells-next-the-Sea. The service operates at roughly 1½–2 hourly intervals on weekdays and Saturdays. The company also runs the CoastHopper service along the A149 between Sheringham (just west of Cromer) and Hunstanton, stopping at Wells-next-the-Sea. This is an hourly service in peak season (June to August) and two-hourly at other times of the year.

> Norfolk Green, Hamlin Way, King's Lynn, Norfolk PE30 4NG Tel: 01553 776980 Fax: 01553 770891 Email: enquiries@norfolkgreen.co.uk Website: www.norfolkgreen.co.uk

Train

The nearest railway stations to Walsingham are at:

Norwich (30 miles), served by *One Railway* with an inter-city connection from London Liverpool Street, and local services in Norfolk and Suffolk. Also *Central Trains* connecting with the Midlands, Manchester and Liverpool via Ely and Peterborough (connecting with East Coast Main Line).

Sheringham (14 miles) *One Railway* local service from Norwich via Wroxham, North Walsham and Cromer.

King's Lynn (25 miles) *First Capital Connect* with direct service from London King's Cross via Cambridge.

> Contact **National Rail Enquiries** (24 hours) on 08457 48 49 50 Website: www.nationalrail.co.uk

The **North Norfolk Railway**, a 'heritage' line with both steam and vintage diesel locomotives, runs from Sheringham to

Holt, where a bus connection can be made with Walsingham (see above). The NNR is primarily a tourist line, so out-of-season services are restricted.

> North Norfolk Railway plc, Sheringham Station, Station Approach, Sheringham, Norfolk NR26 8RA
> Tel: 01263 820800 ('Talking timetable' 01263 820808)
> Fax: 01263 820801
> Email: enquiries@nnrailway.co.uk
> Website: www.nnrailway.co.uk

An unusual way to approach Walsingham is by the **Wells to Walsingham Light Railway**. This 10¼ inch gauge line – said to be the longest in the world of its type – runs from the outskirts of Wells-next-the-Sea (adjacent to the A149 coast road, and close to the B1105 turning) through farmland into the heart of Walsingham, within walking distance of the Shrine and Abbey.

There are five daily services in both directions during August, with four each day in April to July and September, but reducing to three in October. The line is closed at other times.

> Wells to Walsingham Light Railway, Wells-next-the-Sea, Norfolk NR23 1QB Tel: 01328 711630

Air

Norwich International Airport lies on the northern fringe of the city, with scheduled services to and from many destinations around Britain and mainland Europe, in particular Amsterdam Schipol Airport and Mediterranean resorts.

> Norwich International Airport, Amsterdam Way, Norwich NR6 6JA Tel: 01603 411923 Fax: 01603 411923
> Website: www.norwichairport.co.uk

INFORMATION ABOUT THE SHRINES

The Anglican Shrine of Our Lady of Walsingham and the Roman Catholic National Shrine of Our Lady are at the heart of all that draws pilgrims to Walsingham. As well as running the regular worship at the shrines, they offer accommodation and hospitality and organize programmes of events for visitors of all kinds – parties of schoolchildren, students, parish groups, clergy conferences and individual pilgrims making a retreat.

Full and up-to-date details of calendars of events and other activities of the shrine organizations can be found at the official Walsingham website: www.walsingham.org.uk From here you can enter the sites of each shrine to plan your visit, check service times, book accommodation, join one of the pilgrim organizations or shop online.

The Anglican Shrine of Our Lady of Walsingham

The Shrine Office
2 Common Place
Walsingham
Norfolk NR22 6EE
For general enquiries, Tel: 01328 820255, Fax: 01328 824206
Email: accom@olw-shrine.org.uk
Website: www.walsinghamanglican.org.uk

The Anglican Shrine aims to be 'a place of pilgrimage, healing and renewal' and the pilgrimage season runs from Easter to the end of October. Conferences and retreats are run from November to April, when you can also rent cottages in the village. A team led by a 'Pilgrim Hosteler' aims to provide the best possible care of visitors and pilgrims. It is administered by a College of Guardians, which operates on a day-to-day basis as the Walsingham College Trust Association Ltd, a registered charity (No. 215863).

Departments include:

Accommodation Office, 6 Common Place, Walsingham NR22 6BW Tel: 01328 820239 fax and email as above). Most of the accommodation is in the shrine grounds within a short walk of the Shrine itself and the Refectory. Single, twin, double and family rooms are available and a limited number or rooms have disabled access. In addition there are a number of attractive properties in the village available for groups of various sizes. Applications for group bookings are invited from 1 January each year for the *following* year.

Membership, 6 Common Place, Walsingham NR22 6BW
Tel: 01328 820582 Fax: 01328 824206
email: membs@olw-shrine.org.uk

There are a number of associations you can join to support the work and witness of the Anglican Shrine. Enquiries about joining any of these groups should be addressed to the Membership Office.

The Society of Our Lady of Walsingham is the largest association with over 6,500 members who pledge to pray for the Shrine daily.

The Priests Associate of the Holy House has 2,000 members, priests who come to minister at the Shrine with or without their congregations. These priests play a vital role in maintaining daily worship at the Shrine round the year.

The Walsingham Partnership was founded in 2004 to secure the future development of the Shrine. Its members undertake to organize fundraising on behalf of the Shrine.

The Living Rosary of Our Lady of Walsingham is for pilgrims who make a commitment to participate in the rosary as it is recited at Shrine Prayers every day.

Cells of the Holy House of Our Lady of Walsingham is for priests, pilgrim groups and members of the society who meet regularly in their local church to celebrate mass, offer intercessions for the Shrine, arrange fundraising events and plan future pilgrimages.

The Chantry Book. The names of faithful pilgrims now departed can be entered into this book of remembrance which is kept in St Edward's Chapel. They are prayed for in the month of their death and on All Souls Day.

The US Friends of Our Lady of Walsingham
This was set up to make it simpler for American friends of Walsingham to become members of the Society of Priest Associates. Please contact:
The Secretary
US Friends of OLW,
St Paul's Church
2430 K Street, NW,
Washington DC 20037
Email:jhobson@stpauls-kst.com

Education, The College, Knight Street, Walsingham NR22 6EF
Tel: 01328 824205, Fax: 01328 824209
email: ed@olw-shrine.org.uk
Led by a team of qualified and experienced teachers, the Education Department offers a wide variety of RE, history, music, drama and cross-curricular programmes for primary, middle and secondary schools for residential and day visits.

The **Shrine Shop** is also located at 2 Common Place (on the corner with Bridewell Street, opposite the Pump). Tel: 01328 824201, fax: 01328 821654, email: shop@olw-shrine.org.uk
You can also shop online via the website,
http://shop.walsinghamanglican.org.uk/acatalog/

Magazine *The Walsingham Review* is published three times a year and is distributed to members of The Society of Our Lady of Walsingham and Priest Associates. It is also available online via the Shrine's website.

The **Shrine Priest** may be contacted at The College.

The Roman Catholic National Shrine of Our Lady of Walsingham

Pilgrim Bureau
Friday Market Place
Walsingham
Norfolk NR22 6DB
Tel: Bureau 01328 820217, Shrine 01328 820495, Shop 01328 821794
Fax: Bureau 01328 821087, Shop 01328 820174
Website: www.walsingham.org.uk/romancatholic/
Situated about a mile outside Walsingham, the Roman Catholic Shrine complex includes the Slipper Chapel, the Chapel of Reconciliation, the Stations of the Cross and the Annunciation Window. The road that leads to the Shrine from Walsingham is known as the 'holy mile'.

Accommodation Individuals and groups making a pilgrimage to the Roman Catholic Shrine may apply to stay at Elmham House on Friday Market Place, next to the Church of the Annunication. An elegant Georgian building, it was formerly the Walsingham Grammar School, founded in 1639. It has been adapted and extended and now offers comfortable accommodation in single, twin and double rooms. Visitors with special needs can also be accommodated. Bookings may be made by telephone or on line wia the website. Early bookings are strongly advised.

Membership *The Walsingham Assocation* was founded in 1933 to spread devotion to Our Lady of Walsingham and to encourage pilgrims to her Shrine. It currently has over 70 branches in the UK and members receive a quarterly newsletter. For further information, contact the Pilgrim Bureau or email walsinghamassociation@walsingham.org.uk

The Slipper Chapel Bookshop offers visitors a wide selection of books, devotional crafts and gifts. Open daily, it closes between noon and 1 pm for Mass.

WHERE TO STAY

Apart from the accommodation offered by the Anglican and Roman Catholic Shrines, there are numerous other places that pilgrims and visitors can stay in and around Walsingham.

Other accommodation in and around Walsingham

Swallows Restaurant, 15 High Street,
Walsingham, Norfolk NR22 6BY
Tel: 01328 820555

Black Lion Hotel, Friday Market,
Walsingham, Norfolk NR22 6DB
Tel: 01328 820235
Email: lionwalsingham@btconnect.com

Unicorn House, Norwich Road,
Great Snoring, Norfolk NR21 0HR
Tel: 01328 820407

The Old Bakehouse, 33 High Street,
Walsingham, Norfolk NR22 6BZ
Tel and fax: 01328 820454
Email: theoldbakehouseguesthouse@yahoo.co.uk
Website: www.glavenvalley.co.uk/oldbakehouse

The Bull Inn, Common Place,
Walsingham, Norfolk NR22 6BP
Tel: 01328 820333

St David's House, Friday Market,
Walsingham, Norfolk NR22 6BY
Tel: 01328 820633
Email: stdavidshouse@amserve.net
Website: stdavidshousewalsingham.co.uk

Little Way Association,
12 Friday Market, Walsingham, Norfolk NR22 6DB
Tel: 01328 820222

This list is not exhaustive. For other options, including self-catering accommodation, please contact either the Anglican

Shrine or the Pilgrim Bureau for further details, or one of the Tourist Information Offices listed below.

Tourist Information Centres (TICs) in north and north-west Norfolk

Please note: Many of the Tourist Information Centres listed below have restricted opening times outside the main holiday season from Easter to the end of October. However, the Norwich TIC (close to the Market Place and City Hall) remains open throughout the year.

Cromer
Prince of Wales Road, Cromer NR27 9HS
Tel: 01263 512497   Fax: 01263 513613
Email: cromertic@north-norfolk.gov.uk

Holt
3 Pound House, Market Place, Holt NR25 6BW
Tel: 01263 713100   Fax: 01263 713100
Email: holttic@north-norfolk.gov.uk

Hunstanton
Town Hall, The Green, Hunstanton PE36 6BQ
Tel: 01485 532610   Fax: 01485 533972
Email: hunstanton.tic@west-norfolk.gov.uk

King's Lynn
The Custom House, Purfleet Quay, King's Lynn PE30 1HP
Tel: 01553 763044   Fax: 01553 819441
Email: kings-lynn.tic@west-norfolk.gov.uk

Norwich
The Forum, Millennium Plain, Norwich NR2 1TF
Tel: 01603 727927   Fax: 01603 765389
Email: tourism@norwich.gov.uk

Sheringham
Station Approach, Sheringham NR26 8RA
Tel: 01263 824329   Fax: 01263 821668
Email: sheringhamtic@north-norfolk.gov.uk

Wells-next-the-Sea

Staithe Street, Wells-next-the-Sea NR23 1AN

Tel: 01328 710885   Fax: 01328 711405

Email: wellstic@north-norfolk.gov.uk

Walsingham

Shirehall Museum, Common Place, Walsingham NR22 6BP

Tel: 01328 820510   Fax: 01328 820098

Email: walsingham.museum@farmline.com

> The Shirehall at Walsingham was originally part of the
> outer precinct of the Priory. From the mid-eighteenth cen-
> tury until as recently as 1970 it operated as a courthouse,
> before being converted into a fascinating museum of the
> thousand-year history of Walsingham as a place of pilgrim-
> age.

Tourist Information Centres will offer advice on all types of
accommodation available in the areas they serve. There are
also two local trade associations which can be approached.

Hotels of North Norfolk, 22 Holt Road, Cromer,
Norfolk NR29 9JW   Tel: 01263 515900

North Norfolk Hotel and Guest House Association, Mill
Common House, Ridlington, North Walsham, Norfolk
NR28 9TY   Tel: 01692 650792

PLACES OF INTEREST NEAR WALSINGHAM

Wells-next-the-Sea consists of three separate sections, each
of which has its own individual character. The main residential part of the town is grouped around the parish church on
high ground adjacent to the A149 coast road. Of particular
interest is The Buttlands, an attractive tree-fringed green
where medieval archers used to practise, surrounded today
by imposing Georgian and Victorian villas.

Narrow lanes and picturesque alleys – with such nautical
names as Jolly Sailors' Yard and Anchor Lane – drop down
the hillside to a colourful and exuberant quayside with the
usual mix of restaurants, souvenir shops and amusement

11

arcade. Until relatively recently coasters used to load and unload their cargoes of grain, animal feed and coal, but nowadays the harbour provides anchorage for fishing boats and pleasure craft, including the old two-masted Dutch registered sailing clipper *The Albatross* which is a frequent visitor.

A meandering channel runs from the quayside to the open sea over a mile away. Immediately opposite the quay a vast area of salt marsh and winding creeks stretches into the distance, but to the west of the channel a high earthen bank protects the low-lying arable and grazing land beyond. This was reclaimed in the mid nineteenth century by the then Earl of Leicester, whose successors have continued to occupy

the Palladian mansion of Holkham Hall set amidst its huge estate bordering the town to the west. A road on the landward side of the bank gives access to the third part of the town – the beach area. It is this lengthy gap which gives the town its *next-the-sea* suffix! For those who choose

Wells lifeboat shed

Wells quay

not to drive or walk between town and beach, a delightful alternative is the tiny narrow gauge railway running parallel to the road for much of the way. At the seaward end is an extensive caravan and camp site with all amenities, boating lake and large car-park. A pine forest – planted to limit wind erosion – stretches westward along the coast for several miles, shielding the vast expanse of sandy beach. The tide rushes in and out extremely quickly in these shallow waters, and a klaxon sounds to warn bathers and others when the tide turns. It is no coincidence that the Wells lifeboat shed – housing both an inshore rescue and all-weather boat – is located at the junction of beach and channel.

The rapidly expanding town of **Fakenham** lies about 10 miles inland, on a low hill above the unspoilt upper reaches of the River Wensum. The area is thought to have been inhabited since neolithic times, and there is evidence of a Roman settlement at Beacon Hill on the south side of the valley. Fakenham takes its name from the Anglo-Saxon meaning *'fair place'* or perhaps *'place on the fair river'*, and had a population of

Market day at Fakenham

150 when surveyed for the Domesday Book in 1086. A curious feature of the present-day town is the number of small 'island' groups of buildings. These may well be survivors of disastrous fires in the seventeenth and eighteenth centuries.

A charter was granted in 1250 for a market which continues to this day. Thursday is market day, when the town centre in the shadow of the fourteenth-century parish church is thronged with stalls selling a vast array of goods from fruit and vegetables to clothing, plants and household supplies. A large sale yard and adjacent auction room attract vendors and buyers – as well as the merely curious – from far and wide. A recent venture is the Farmers' Market held on the fourth Saturday of every month. As befits the largest town in the area serving much of north Norfolk, there are excellent amenities including a wide range of shops – including many national chains – department stores and supermarkets.

Just outside the town centre is the former gasworks which ceased operating in 1965. It is believed to be the only surviving works remaining in England and Wales, and is home to the Museum of Gas and Local Industry. Another claim to fame is the well-known race-course with its superb modern Prince of Wales Stand, just south of the town. Around ten days of racing – mainly steeplechasing and point-to-point – are held each year.

With only fragmentary remains, it is difficult to appreciate the scale and extent of Walsingham Abbey, but a visit to nearby **Binham Priory** provides some evidence. Binham lies about 4 miles north-east of Walsingham, close to the A149 coast road. The Benedictine Priory was founded in 1091, but following the Dissolution in the early sixteenth century most of the nave was retained as the village parish church. Although much of the rest has disappeared, the lower sections of wall and foundations have been preserved to make the overall layout – similar in many respects to Walsingham – clearly discernible.

Walsingham is well placed for exploring the Norfolk countryside and north Norfolk coast, with the picturesque villages of Burnham Market, Morston and Blakeney close by. Also worth exploring are Holt, Sheringham and Cromer.

Nearby are Holkham and Houghton Halls. Sandringham, Oxburgh, Felbrigg and Blickling are somewhat further away but easily accessible by car.

LOCAL INFORMATION

There are two local newspapers:

Eastern Daily Press (regional morning, Monday–Saturday) Prospect House, Rouen Road, Norwich NR1 1RE
Tel: 01603 628311
Available from newsagents and street vendors throughout the region.

North Norfolk News (local weekly) 31 Church Street, Cromer, Norfolk NR27 9ES   Tel: 01263 513232
Available from newsagents or by subscription.

2

The Story of Walsingham

How it all began

Seal of Walsingham Priory

The story of how Walsingham became a place of pilgrimage is enshrined in an old ballad (called the 'Pynson Ballad' after its printer, Richard Pynson), written many years after the events it purports to speak of actually took place. But the outline of the story may be taken as factual, giving rise, as it did, to a wonderful flowering of faith which inspires people even to this day.

In 1061, so the story goes (although it is generally thought by historians to have taken place several decades later), the lady of the manor of Little Walsingham, a widow named Richeldis de Faverches, prayed to Our Lady asking how she could honour her in some special way. In answer to this prayer Mary led Richeldis in spirit to Nazareth and showed her the house in which she had first received the angel's message.

Mary told Richeldis to take the measurements of this house and build another one just like it in Walsingham. It would be a place where people could come to honour Mary and her

Son, remembering especially the mystery of the Annunciation and Mary's joyful 'Yes' to conceiving the Saviour.

Richeldis immediately set about erecting a small wooden chapel measuring 23 feet 6 inches by 12 feet 10 inches, in accordance with our Lady's instructions. However, the legend relates that on the first of two possible sites chosen the builders could not get the pieces to fit together and went home disheartened. After a night spent in prayer, Richeldis found that angels had raised the holy house on the second site, and there it remained for posterity. Richeldis herself loved to pray in this little house-chapel, remembering the first holy house in Nazareth and Jesus' growing years in an ordinary family home.

The late eleventh century and all through the twelfth and thirteenth century was the era of the crusades, which saw a growing interest in the sites consecrated by the human presence of Jesus in the Holy Land. But now pilgrims need not go so far; in England itself there was a 'new Nazareth' built by one of their own countrywomen.

The widow's son, Geoffrey, when he himself was later about to depart on crusade, left his mother's precious chapel in the care of a priest-guardian; he wanted it to be safely preserved since Mary herself had asked for it. Later a community of Augustinian canons established themselves on the site and enclosed the original wooden house within their great priory church. It became a 'little house within a great house of God'. A statue of Our Lady with the Child on her knee was set up in the place of honour, showing Mary 'at home' in her own dwelling.

Soon pilgrims began to come and pray in the holy house, not only from the Norfolk area but from all over England and even abroad. Many kings and queens came on pilgrimage too, beginning with Henry III in 1226, followed by his son Edward I, who had a special love for Our Lady of Walsingham. Records show that countless royal and noble men and women travelled to Walsingham, and besides the aristocracy there were numerous ordinary pilgrims, many hoping for a cure of mind or body, others to give thanks for deliverance from danger on land or sea. Thanks to Our Lady of

Walsingham, England became known as Our Lady's Dowry, so much did the people of this land show their love for the Mother of God.

On big feasts the holy house would be lit up by hundreds of candles as pilgrims thronged to pray. It was as if Nazareth had been reincarnated in England. The little wooden house and its statue became the focus of a devotion that reached far beyond the shores of this island. All this was due to a shrine, situated in the beautiful Norfolk countryside and built by an unassuming widow so long ago.

The Pynson Ballad

This account of the founding of Walsingham is the only medieval document we have telling of the Shrine's beginnings. It was printed by Richard Pynson in 1493 but most likely dates from around 1465. The documents and books referred to in the ballad have now all been lost.

This is a modern and slightly adapted rendering of the story.

This chapel was founded
in the year 1061,
during the reign of Saint Edward, King of our land.

All you spiritual people devoted to this place,
coming to ask Our Lady's help
in all kinds of trouble and need,
you can learn how this chapel came into existence
by reading the story of a miracle as recounted below.

A noble widow, sometime lady of this place,
a woman of virtuous life whose name was Richeldis,
asked Our Lady if she could honour her
in some special way.
The Blessed Virgin granted this prayer
in the manner I shall describe,
asking her to build this chapel in her memory.

Our Lady led Richeldis in spirit to Nazareth
and showed her the house where the angel had greeted
    her.
'Look, daughter' said Our Lady.
'Take the measurements of this house
and erect another one like it in Walsingham,
dedicated to praising and honouring me.
All who come there shall find help in their need.

'It shall be a perpetual memorial
to the great joy of the Annunciation,
ground and origin of all my joys
and the root of humanity's gracious redemption.
This came about through Gabriel's message
that I would be a mother through my humility,
and conceive God's Son in virginity.'

The devout woman saw this vision three times.
She gladly took note of the measurements of the building,
    thanking our Lady
for the grace that never deserts the needy.
That very same hour she called workmen together
to build the chapel Our Lady had asked for.

That night a meadow was soaked
with heavenly dew sent down by Mary.
Only two places were marked as her choice
for on them no dew had fallen. They remained dry.
This was the first intimation
of where our new Nazareth should stand,
built like the first in the Holy Land.

When everything was ready
Richeldis remained in a quandary.
Which of the two places shown by Our Lady
should be chosen for her house
since both areas were equal in circumference?
For there were two miraculous dry places in the dew
as Gideon's fleece had likewise remained dry.

The widow thought that the best choice
would be to erect Our Lady's house
where the chapel of St Lawrence now stands
by the twin wells.
Visitors to the place know it well.

The carpenters set to work, digging the foundations
on which the holy house would rise.
But they were soon baffled by the fact
that nothing seemed to fit together properly despite all
    their careful reckoning.
They felt very discouraged at this failure
for they could not account for it naturally.

At last they laid down their tools
and Richeldis told them to go off and rest.
She was confident that Our Lady,
who was the initiator of the work in hand,
would bring it to completion in her own way.
For this Richeldis prayed earnestly.

All night the widow remained in prayer;
while our blessed Lady, the chief architect,
raised the house by the hands of angels
and set it two hundred feet or more
from the original site.
Books mention this.

When the builders returned in the morning
to continue their work,
they found every part of the building faultlessly joined,
far better than anything they could have done themselves.
So each man returned to his own home,
and the holy woman thanked Our Lady
for the great favour she had shown her.

Since then Our Lady has performed many miracles here,
too many to recount in a short space.
For more than four hundred years
chronicles bear witness

that those who visit Mary's house on pilgrimage
are, as it were, daily showered with grace.

Many sick have been cured by Our Lady's power,
the dead revived, the lame made whole,
the blind have had their sight restored.
Sailors have been brought safely to port
through tempest and storm.
Deaf-mutes, lunatics and lepers have all been made well
through Our Lady's intercession.

People troubled by evil spirits
have experienced deliverance.
Also souls suffering from inner problems
have found comfort.
Every human suffering, bodily or spiritual,
can find a remedy here
by devoutly calling upon Our Lady.

Therefore, pilgrims all,
strive to serve Our Lady with humble love.
Apply yourself to doing as she would wish,
remembering the great joy of her Annunciation.
This brief ballad,
though lacking in rhythm and eloquence,
has been written in her honour.

Educated folk with greater intelligence
can learn more about the founding of this chapel
by consulting learned books.
Chronicles about it can help you understand
the whole history and circumstances surrounding this
    place,
for they bear witness to it.

O England, You have every reason to be glad
that you are compared to the promised land of Sion.
This glorious Lady's grace and favour
attest that you can be called everywhere
the holy land, Our Lady's Dowry,
a name given to you from of old.

This title is due to the fact
that here is built the house of new Nazareth
in honour of our heavenly Queen
and her glorious Salutation.
As Gabriel hailed her with an 'Ave' in old Nazareth
so here that is daily remembered with joy.

O gracious Lady, glory of Jerusalem,
cypress of Sion and Joy of Israel,
Rose of Jericho and Star of Bethlehem,
O glorious Lady, do not deny our requests
for you are the most merciful of all women.
Therefore, blessed Lady, grant your great grace
to all who devoutly visit this place.

The Widow Richeldis

Who was Richeldis? How we would love to know more about
this woman at the start of Walsingham's story. From her sur-
name she was possibly an Anglo-Saxon woman married to a
foreigner, one of the conqueror's men, so despite her seem-
ing wealth and social position she would have been counted
among the biblical 'little ones', people who have to depend
on God, not self, for their meaning. Widows had a hard life
whatever their country or situation, and we know Richeldis
had a son to support. No wonder she turned to the Mother
of God in prayer.

Throughout Christian history Marian shrines have been the
result of God's choice of the unlikely candidate: Bernadette,
the asthmatic illiterate of Lourdes, the shepherds of Fatima,
Mariette Beco of Banneaux, daughter of an unemployed and

irreligious labourer, and known for her own sharp tongue. And those who respond to Mary's presence are mainly the poor who reach out to symbols of hope, the hope that God is concerned for them in their sickness and need, that they have a value even if they do not count in the corridors of power.

Like the widow of Luke's Gospel who gave 'all that she had', even if only a widow's mite, so Richeldis gave 'all that she had' to honour another woman: a woman who had been a joyful girl at the Annunciation, but also a wife and widow, the mother of a son as Richeldis herself had been.

Richeldis had asked for a way to honour Our Lady, but she was open as regards to means. What could she do? She sought God's will in prayer and meditation. Hers is the story not so much of a vision but of human search and co-operation with grace. Nowhere indeed is a vision cited as the miracle of Walsingham. It is the siting and raising of the house that constitutes the special sign of Mary's visitation.

Richeldis as founder is so transparent that she literally fades into the background once her task is accomplished. She is a woman who knew all the seasons of a woman's life experience: girlhood and virginity, wifehood, human fruitfulness in maternity, deprivation and barrenness in the widowed state. She does not even have the 'richness' of being proclaimed a saint. There appears to have been no spontaneous veneration of her person as one who had 'seen' Our Lady, no cult of her sanctity, no tradition that she later entered religious life or took up residence near her chapel as an anchoress. Indeed it is very possible from other documents we have that she remarried. We simply do not know for sure.

Richeldis is born, grows, marries, becomes a mother, then a widow. She is used by God for a certain work. She dies. Maybe she was not even particularly holy. Nevertheless, she stands as a symbol of the countless women who have 'done what they could' for God and been content. Therefore the place in which she honoured the Mother of God has become a holy place, a 'new Nazareth' for countless generations, ready to proclaim with Mary in her Magnificat that 'God has done great things for me, holy is his name, and his mercy is on those who fear him from generation to generation.'

The Symbol of the House

The house – image of Mary the Virgin

Richeldis had arranged for a house to be built at Walsingham on the pattern of Mary's house at Nazareth – a perpetual reminder of the joy she experienced at the Annunciation. Here two themes are held in tension: the theme of stability and security symbolized by the house, and the theme of openness to the Spirit – a readiness for change and the unexpected, for the welcome of new life as depicted in the story of the Annunciation.

At the heart of Christianity lies the mystery of the incarnation, 'the Word was made flesh and lived among us'. It was Mary's preparedness that enabled her to receive the seed of the Word, that Jesus might grow within her, become literally 'flesh of her flesh'.

At the beginning of his human life Jesus, like all infants, needed a place to come to, a place within his mother's womb and a place of nurture at Nazareth. He too needed house and home. The home is the 'womb' from which we are all born into the wider society, and Jesus too needed to be part of a human family through being part of a family at Nazareth.

So the house at Walsingham is a symbol of Mary herself, for it not only commemorates her trustful 'Yes' to the angel's message but is a picture of who she was. Mary the virgin was empty, waiting in readiness to become the dwelling place of the Son.

Mary is the virginal house built by God himself to receive the Word made flesh. Her emptiness and expectancy are rooted deeply in her nation's religious faith and history. In her own body she bears the hopes and yearning of many generations of the Jewish people. She is the one who will open the Abrahamic and Davidic promises to the world.

Mary was enabled to say 'Yes' because she had empty space within her to be filled. She was ready to welcome the Word because she had deep security in her identity. She personified a people led by the Lord at every point of their history. Our Lady, the Lightbearer, carries the Light for all.

The house – image of Mary as mother

The house is also an image of Mary as mother, for from the beginning Walsingham was identified with the home in which Jesus spent his growing years, with Mary at its heart, as a mother is at the heart of every home.

At Nazareth Jesus received his first taste of love's sweetness within an ordinary Jewish home. So the holy house at Walsingham stands for the sanctity of family life. Each home is to be a holy house where the Word becomes flesh once more among those who live there.

The Gospels tell us little of the early life of Jesus, but we can surmise much from the picture they convey of his mother and foster father, and from the portrayal of the adult man Jesus became. During his ministry he spoke with the confidence of a truly free person. He withdrew often for nights of solitary prayer. He was drawn upon unceasingly by the multitude of sick and needy around him. Such a life could only be borne if his roots were deep. To be loved and secure in love is the only way people can live deeply and confidently. Because Jesus had been 'at home' in Nazareth he was able to live fully, and trust the Father confidently, anywhere.

In seeing the house as an image of Mary the mother it reflects her stability, solidity, selfless love and practical devotion, taking place within the context of a Jewish home where the mother held an honoured place. A house which is a true home needs expanding walls to accommodate friends, relatives and travellers and we must never forget the Jewish love of 'getting together' with the extended family. It is no coincidence that medieval Walsingham had a special place assigned to St Anne, mother of the Mother of God, grandmother of Jesus.

The house – image of every Christian

Richeldis' empty wooden house was a means of bringing to the minds of pilgrims the kind of person Mary was when she uttered her 'Yes'' to motherhood – a woman empty, poor, yet receptive and joyful in that poverty and virginity.

The goal of the pilgrim, then, is to come to Mary's house and there stand symbolically in her shoes and utter a personal 'Yes' to God in the context of each one's own life. It is to become like Mary a house of God, a hearer of the Word and a bearer of the Spirit.

At Walsingham I put myself in Mary's place, stand in her home and utter her 'Yes' to my own life, and my own call to be a new house of God, a new Nazareth in my own person and my own place. May Mary pray for us that we receive this grace to be Christbearers in our turn, for that is life's greatest happiness.

The Annunciation

The mystery of the Annunciation stands in contradistinction to the symbol of the house. The house is the image of stability. To build is to create something destined to endure beyond one's own lifespan. Therefore building is always an act of hope. It speaks of trust in the future; indeed a certainty that there will be a future.

Richeldis' house perpetuates her memory. It symbolizes the permanence of the Church enduring from generation to generation. It roots Nazareth in England – now and for years ahead. It is a perpetual memorial.

A statue can be moved around, not so a house. It was the little wooden house that made Nazareth permanently present in Walsingham, standing firm and strong, guaranteeing the future of the village and Shrine.

But this is balanced by the theme of the Annunciation which implies a radical openness to change and growth. Every one of us carries within ourselves an element of unpredictability. We are not machines to be manipulated, but free persons able to respond and to choose. Mary's future did not unfold as she had planned or expected, just as Walsingham's own history must surely have developed in a way that Richeldis did not and could not foresee.

Richeldis gave momentum to something bigger than herself and her own private piety, just as Mary gave birth to a Son whose future was not in her own hands. All life, real life, is unpredictable. Stability should prepare us for change or it becomes mere stagnation.

As she is presented to us at the beginning of Luke's Gospel, Mary stands for the perfect disciple. Like Israel of old, she is called and chosen simply out of love. She has not chosen God, rather God has chosen her. She is a child of grace, of choice, and so she is able to respond to God's initiative with the words 'Behold the handmaid of the Lord; be it done to me according to your word.'

But that is not the end of the story. Mary had to be open to human growth and development, just as Jesus had to grow physically, spiritually, socially. She had to make choices, accept responsibility, and ultimately let her Son go his own way even when she did not understand.

Trust implies a readiness to venture into the unknown, secure in a love greater than oneself and one's own limited plans. So we see that at the centre of Walsingham is a specific woman, Mary, who listened to God and said 'Yes' from the depths of her being, a woman who handed herself over so completely that God could fulfil the Divine Will in her. In and through her a new future was inaugurated for the human race. Pondering on the Annunciation we can see that Mary's attitude encapsulates the Christian vocation of us all – to listen, to love and to bear life.

To listen

Mary at the Annunciation is shown as the attentive one. When the angel speaks to her she is ready to respond and take part in the dialogue. But that is one moment picked out of many others that have led up to this point and will lead from it. Mary had to face a future that included bewilderment and pain. She had to ponder things in her heart. There were times when she did not understand, such as the time Jesus was lost in Jerusalem at the age of twelve. There was even a time when relatives thought Jesus was out of his mind. Still Mary clung on, and at the end was found standing at the foot of the cross – sorrowful, yet still faithful.

'Blessed are those who hear the word of God and keep it.' This is the core of discipleship – hearing and keeping the word as it is revealed to us at every moment and in every event. It means walking by faith, not sight; fostering an attentive attitude, ready for the unexpected and the challenging. But on the whole we don't want to listen and be challenged, we would rather life unfolded in a predictable manner that left us feeling in charge and able to cope.

Listening is to be attentive not only to God in prayer but to life itself. And to listen with Mary's attitude is to hear the answer to the question 'What is being asked of me now . . . in this situation? What is God saying to me in this happiness, this sorrow, this illness, this affliction, this antipathy? What is God saying in these dry prayers when I can't think even one good thought?' If we truly believe that God can speak to us in all the events of life, working all things for good, we will be able to say 'Yes' to our lives as they unfold, often in unexpected ways.

To love

Mary is inseparable from the idea of Christian love. To make love our life project, as Mary did, means for each one to cultivate an inner virginity, an openness and availability to the Divine. It is to have a sense of one's own integrity and eschew over-dependence on others to give life meaning. But conversely it is also motherliness – nurturing others through affirmation and challenge according to each one's capacities.

The more we know others the more we grow to love them, and growing in knowledge is hard work. That is why laziness is the antithesis of love. Love always makes the effort to know more so as to love and understand more. Mary had to constantly extend herself in faith, in commitment to the unfolding Word of God – in the flesh, in Scripture, and in her daily life choices.

Even if our love is hidden within our own small environment it is never wasted. People who love and are loved increase their capacity for love. Each of us can, if we wish, be 'Love in the heart of the Church' just as Mary's love was at the heart of Nazareth. If we look at Mary we see a committed love – strong, selfless, mature. 'Be it done unto me . . .' I offer myself for whatever you want.

Prayer stretches our capacity for love, enabling us to love an ever greater number of people, take all the world's sorrow and pain to our hearts. It is through the knowledge of our own weakness that we understand how vulnerable each person is, how easily wounded, how much in need of understanding. Mary is the mother of mercy and compassion now, just as she was to those early pilgrims who came to Walsingham seeking healing, and enabling them in their turn to give healing to a fractured and broken world. Love incarnate in deed – in patience, kindness, tenderness – is the only love that really counts. The rest is mere wishful thinking.

To bear life

People who love should be fully alive, radiant with the Lord, and therefore creative, life-bestowing persons. Mary is so fully alive because she bears life in all its fulness as a result of her 'Fiat' ('Be it done unto me').

Our common Christian vocation is also to give life by bearing Jesus within ourselves. We have to allow him to be conceived in us, formed in us, So that we can offer him to others in our turn.

Living fully is the result of loving and listening. In Jesus and Mary we see people fully alive, fully loving. It is a great pity if religious men and women strike others as being only half alive; it is a sign that something has gone wrong.

Mary is our model as one who responded totally, allowed God to do with her all that he wanted. When Jesus says that his mother, brothers and sisters are those who do the will of his Father in heaven we have a glimpse of the wholeness of Mary's self-giving, her detachment, her ability to let her son 'be' in freedom, a glimpse too into what made Mary the woman she was. It was not bearing Christ in the flesh that made her blessed. Her real motherhood lay in her surrender to the Father's will; her 'Fiat' in sorrow and in joy, in diminishment and fulness.

Walsingham exists to remind us of the mystery of Mary's silent surrender, her self-sacrificing love, her joy and humility in bearing and believing the Word of God.

The Spirit is ultimate freedom, total unpredictability. God lives not in a 'house made with hands' but in hearts that are, with Mary, ready for anything – 'Be it done unto me according to your word.'

Restoration and Renewal

Walsingham remained one of Europe's premier shrines until the Reformation, becoming extremely wealthy in the process. Henry VIII came here to give thanks for the birth of a son by Katherine of Aragon, his first wife. But the infant later died, and Henry, in his desire for a male heir, was soon to seek another bride.

In the aftermath of Henry's break with Rome came the Dissolution of the monasteries and other religious houses, among them the Priory at Walsingham in 1538. The ancient Shrine was destroyed and the statue of Our Lady burned at Smithfield. The holy house was levelled to the ground and the beautiful priory church was left to fall into ruins. Most people forgot that the place had once known a constant stream of pilgrims.

Then in 1875 the Pynson Ballad (see p. 18) was discovered and reprinted. Interest in Our Lady of Walsingham was thus revived among both Anglicans and Roman Catholics. The Priory grounds were partially excavated and the ancient seal of Our Lady of Walsingham published, showing on one side the Augustinian church and on the other the image of Mary seated on a high-backed throne with the Child on her lap holding a book of the Gospels. Beneath Mary's feet was a toadstone, an old East Anglian symbol of evil.

In 1894 a Miss Charlotte Boyd discovered the ancient Slipper Chapel, now abutting a dwelling and used as a barn. At her own expense she restored the chapel and gifted it to the Roman Catholic Diocese of Northampton. A replica of the holy house in miniature was erected in the Roman Catholic

Church of the Annunciation at King's Lynn (in which parish the village of Walsingham was situated at that time) and from there took place, in 1897, the first pilgrimage to Walsingham since the Reformation. After that interest waned, and the Slipper Chapel stood well cared for but empty.

Meanwhile in 1921 a new vicar, Alfred Hope Patten, was appointed to the Anglican living of Walsingham, and he was determined to reawaken love for Mary in her own village. He had a statue made for the parish church according to the pattern of the original Priory seal. This statue was installed in the Guild's Chapel of the Anglican Church of St Mary on 16 July 1922. Parishioners began to gather there each evening to pray the rosary and offer other prayers of intercession. The custom of what has come to be called Shrine Prayers has never lapsed since that time.

In 1931 a separate Shrine Church was erected, and within it was placed a holy house similar to the one revealed to Richeldis, but this time built of brick rather than wood. The statue was carried to it in procession and enthroned above the altar. A well, uncovered when the foundations were being laid, is now within the main Shrine Church, and is used for a daily service of sprinkling pilgrims with holy water.

Around the same time the Slipper Chapel, located one mile from the village, was reopened and began to be used for worship by Roman Catholic pilgrims. An additional chapel was dedicated to the Holy Spirit' and in 1982 the beautiful Chapel of Reconciliation, patterned on a Norfolk barn, was built to accommodate the growing number of pilgrims. The Slipper Chapel, like the Anglican Shrine, has a statue of Our Lady in a place of honour, carved to the medieval seal design. The Slipper Chapel has since been designated as the English National Shrine of Our Lady, and both Shrines have seen a steady growth of pilgrims.

It was the Second Vatican Council that opened the way for better ecumenical relationships between Christians of different denominations. Now the staff and directors of both Shrines meet and worship together on a regular basis. In fact, the village has become one shrine-village with two focal points, the Anglican Shrine Church and the Slipper Chapel, with two Orthodox chapels also in the vicinity. The Priory grounds have remained in private hands. No one Church has exclusive access to them, and it seems right that all of the big pilgrimages can enter the grounds and, under the ruins of the great east window, celebrate the Eucharist and pray at the site of the original holy house. Mary has come back to Walsingham, bringing her Child with her, and the presence of both is felt once more in the village of her choice.

In Walsingham today the mystery of the incarnation again becomes a reality as the Angelus bell rings out in memory of the Annunciation. Here Nazareth is recalled and the sanctity of family life upheld. Here in silent prayer and public praise pilgrims can experience love and acceptance, healing and wholeness. Above all they are summoned to rejoice with Mary and echo her 'Yes' in their own lives – that in them too the Word may become flesh and dwell in today's world through their presence.

The Statue of Our Lady of Walsingham

The present statue of Our Lady of Walsingham in the Roman Catholic Shrine is fashioned according to the design on the medieval Priory seal.

A modern interpretation of the image is as follows.

- Mary is seated on a throne, and is crowned to denote her queenship.
- The throne has two pillars, symbolizing either the pillars of the House of God or the twofold pillars of the Old Covenant, love of God and neighbour.
- There are seven rings on the pillars, three on one side and four on the other, to remind the pilgrim of the Seven Sacraments. Between the

Statue of Our Lady of Walsingham, Slipper Chapel

33

pillars the arch is in the shape of a rainbow, the sign of God's unfailing Covenant with every living creature at the time of Noah (Gen. 9.12).

- Beneath the throne is a toadstone, ancient symbol of evil, for Mary has overcome the ancient curse of Genesis and is the New Eve.
- Mary holds a threefold lily sceptre, symbol of her virginity and sovereignty.
- Mary presents to us her Child, holding a book of the Gospels.
- Jesus, the Word made flesh, enthroned on the lap of his Mother, Seat of Wisdom, extends his arm in a double gesture of blessing the onlooker and protecting his mother.

The statue in the Slipper Chapel was taken to Wembley Stadium and occupied a place of honour on the altar when Pope John Paul II celebrated Mass there in 1982.

It is one of the few Marian statues to be crowned in the name of the Pope. Our Lady of Walsingham was officially crowned during the Marian Year 1954 on the feast of the Assumption.

Today, at the Dowry of Mary Pilgrimage in September, a replica of the statue is carried by sisters of the new Community of Our Lady of Walsingham based at the House of Prayer in Brentwood.

3

What to See and Where to Go

THE ROMAN CATHOLIC SHRINE

Walsingham is very much the village and the Shrine combined. There are two main Shrines, one belonging to the Anglican Church and the other belonging to the Roman Catholic Church. Pilgrims to Walsingham will usually visit both places, as well as enjoying the village with its many shops and tea rooms, and the 'Abbey' grounds where the remains of the medieval Priory and site of the original holy house can be seen.

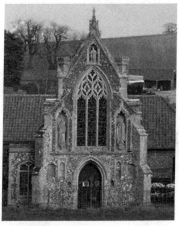

For the sake of ease this guide will begin with the Slipper Chapel and the Roman Catholic Shrine, and then move into the village for the Anglican Shrine and guide to other churches in the area. The Roman Catholic Shrine, comprising the Slipper Chapel, the Chapel of the Holy Spirit and the Chapel of Reconciliation, is situated a mile from the village of Little Walsingham.

The Slipper Chapel

The Slipper Chapel

The Slipper Chapel was built some time around 1338 and is dedicated to St Catherine of Alexandria, patron saint of pilgrims to the Holy Land. It was constructed in such a way that the sun rose directly behind the altar on her feast day, 25 November.

Here, in medieval times, the pilgrims would confess their sins, then remove their shoes and walk the last 'holy mile' into Walsingham barefoot. Henry VIII presumably stopped here when he was en route to Walsingham to give thanks for the birth of a son in January 1511. Unfortunately the child died in February of the same year, and it was Henry who was later responsible for the Shrine's destruction.

After the Dissolution of the Monasteries the Slipper Chapel fell into disuse, being used as a private dwelling and later as a cow barn. It was purchased and restored by Miss Charlotte Boyd in 1894 and given to the Benedictines of Downside, but no services were permitted to be held here. However, in 1930 a new Bishop of Northampton took an interest in the chapel and had it refurbished and decorated in medieval English style. It was opened officially in 1934, since when it has been designated the National Marian Shrine for Roman Catholics in England.

The altar, richly carved and painted by local artists Lilian and James Dagless, shows St Lawrence (one of the patrons of

The altar of the Slipper Chapel

the ancient Walsingham Priory) and St Catherine of Alexandria. The statue of Our Lady of Walsingham, to the left of the altar and under a high canopy, is the focus of devotion. There are two stained glass windows: the one above the altar by Geoffrey Webb commemorates the definition of the dogma of the Assumption in 1950. The one at the back of the chapel depicts the Annunciation by Alfred Fisher, and was a gift

GROUNDS of the SLIPPER CHAPEL R.C. SHRINE

Chapel of Reconciliation

Open Air Sanctuary

Way of the Cross

HOLY MILE ⇨ to Walsingham village

Priest's House

Slipper Chapel

Cloister

Chapel of The Holy Spirit

Holy Water Fountain

Shops, offices and amenities

from the Guild of Our Lady of Ransom to celebrate the centenary of modern pilgrimage in 1997.

The Chapel of the Holy Spirit

The Chapel of the Holy Spirit, together with the adjoining sacristy, was built in 1938, and is connected to the Slipper Chapel by a short cloister. It has been completely redesigned as a chapel for burning candles in honour of Our Lady. The focal point is a fine mosaic by the Jewish artist Anna Wyner, depicting Mary in the midst of the apostles on the day of Pentecost.

Mary, as Mother of the Church, prays with us, for us, and as one of us, that we too may be filled with the spirit of Jesus and be ready to proclaim his Name to others.

The Chapel of Reconciliation

The Chapel of Reconciliation, built according to the pattern of a Norfolk barn to blend in with the surrounding countryside, is dark and silent within, its plain brick, steel and warm-toned wood inviting the pilgrim to meditation and prayer.

The church was dedicated in 1982 and can accommodate a large number of people. The wall behind the main altar has been designed in such a way that it can be opened out for greater gatherings, which include crowds in the open air. The icon to the left of the altar was commissioned by a former director of the Shrine and painted by a monk of the Russian Orthodox Church. To the right the Blessed Sacrament is reserved.

The theme of reconciliation and Christian unity is one which calls forth the longing in many hearts that Walsingham may be a centre for all Christians to unite in their love for Jesus and his Mother.

Throughout the year a Pilgrimage Mass is celebrated daily at noon in the Chapel of Reconciliation, and there is an afternoon period of adoration of the Blessed Sacrament.

The Shrine Gardens

Outside in the grounds a Way of the Cross, a holy water fountain, tea room, shop and picnic facilities help to make the place an attractive space for both prayer and enjoyment.

For full details of services and pilgrimages contact The Pilgrim Bureau, details on p. 8.

WALSINGHAM VILLAGE

The Anglican Shrine

The Anglican Shrine Church in the village of Little Walsingham was built by Father Hope Patten in 1931 and contains a replica of the original holy house. It is a real 'people's church', many local artists and craftsmen and women being responsible for its decoration and adornment. Special mention must be made of the fine murals by Enid Chadwick.

The large ceramic picture that meets the eye of every pilgrim entering the church is a copy of Andrea della Robbia's terracotta of the Annunciation in the sanctuary of La Verna,

The Anglican Shrine

Statue of Our Lady of Walsingham, robed, Anglican Chapel

The altar of the Anglican Shrine

where St Francis of Assisi received the stigmata, or wounds of Christ. The Annunciation is the primary mystery commemorated at Walsingham.

The holy house which contains the statue of Our Lady of Walsingham, robed on feast days, is built of brick, with inlaid pieces of stone from the sites of many abbeys and holy places in England. Within, candles burn continually as a reminder of perpetual prayer.

The Shrine Church contains many interesting statues, as well as 15 small chapels, each one dedicated to a mystery of the rosary. The last chapel, dedicated to the Crowning of Our Lady as Queen of Heaven, is situated upstairs, and is a place where the Sacrament is reserved for quiet prayer and private meditation.

A well discovered during the Shrine's construction provides

Walsingham Village

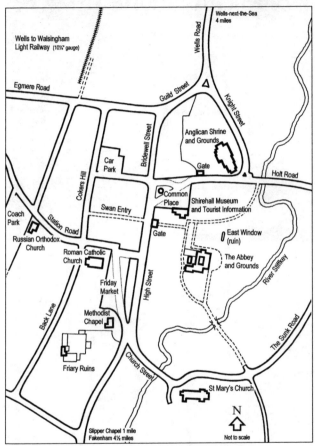

a constant supply of water for blessing and healing purposes, and is a reminder to the pilgrim of his or her baptismal promises.

By the main door can be seen tablets inscribed with thanks for prayers at the Shrine which have been answered.

ᴛʜᴇ ᴀɴɢʟɪᴄᴀɴ ꜱʜʀɪɴᴇ ᴄʜᴜʀᴄʜ

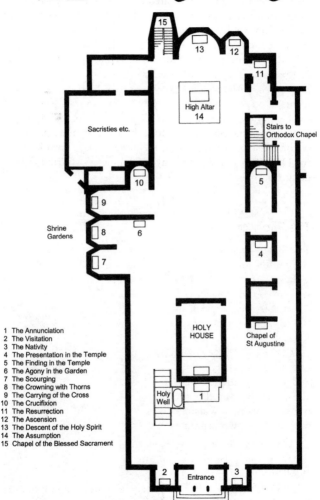

15

13   12

11

High Altar
14

Sacristies etc.

Stairs to
Orthodox Chapel

10

5

9

8   6

Shrine
Gardens

4

7

HOLY
HOUSE

Chapel of
St Augustine

Holy
Well   1

2   Entrance   3

1 The Annunciation
2 The Visitation
3 The Nativity
4 The Presentation in the Temple
5 The Finding in the Temple
6 The Agony in the Garden
7 The Scourging
8 The Crowning with Thorns
9 The Carrying of the Cross
10 The Crucifixion
11 The Resurrection
12 The Ascension
13 The Descent of the Holy Spirit
14 The Assumption
15 Chapel of the Blessed Sacrament

The Shrine grounds

The Shrine grounds contain an outdoor Way of the Cross, a pond and fountain, and a newly opened quiet garden. There is also an outdoor altar (dedicated to the new rosary Mysteries of Light) for large pilgrimages, and another chapel dedicated to the Holy Souls. The surroundings are conducive to prayer and reflection and a warm welcome awaits all visitors.

Within the Shrine grounds is the Priory where the sisters of the Society of St Margaret live. They help with the sacristy work, with the spiritual guidance of pilgrims, and other forms of pastoral outreach.

There is accommodation for pilgrims on site, and an excellent educational programme for schools and young people.

For a list of service times, including Mass, Sprinkling at the Holy Well and Shrine Prayers, contact the Shrine Office, details on p. 5.

The Priory or 'Abbey'

The Priory was originally founded in 1153 and housed a community of Augustinian canons who cared for pilgrims. They built a magnificent church within which the holy house was enshrined.

After the Dissolution of the Monasteries by Henry VIII the buildings fell into ruin because, unlike many other places where abbey and priory churches were subsequently used for parish worship, Walsingham had its own separate parish church.

The site of the former Augustinian Priory is at the top of the High Street, but the way in, except on

Walsingham · Priory

Plan of the medieval Augustinian Priory (now known locally as 'the Abbey'). All that is left of the great Church is the arch of the east window. The site of the original holy house is marked by a small stone slab set in the ground.

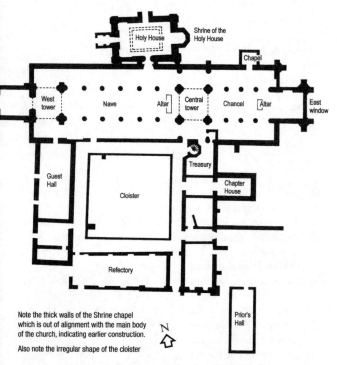

Note the thick walls of the Shrine chapel which is out of alignment with the main body of the church, indicating earlier construction.

Also note the irregular shape of the cloister

pilgrimage days, is through the Shirehall Museum entrance in the Common Place. The site is in private hands and the former Priory is mostly a ruin, although there are some well-preserved remains, especially the great arch of the east window. On most days of the year the grounds are open to visitors and pilgrims at stated times. The site of the original holy house is marked with a cross set in the ground, and beyond the great arch can be seen the holy wells and stone bath, presumably used for immersing the sick in former times under the patronage of St Lawrence.

As you pass through to the Abbey grounds there is an interesting small museum, photograph collection and Victorian courthouse accessible to the public.

If the grounds are closed, the great arch can be viewed from the far end of the churchyard in St Mary's Church on the Sunk Road.

The ruins of the medieval Franciscan Friary, just before you reach the High Street from the Roman Catholic Shrine, are also in private hands, and are the best preserved Franciscan ruins in England. They are seldom accessible to the public, but can be clearly seen from the road.

 ## The Parish church of St Mary and All Saints

St Mary's Church is built on the original Saxon site that Richeldis and her son Geoffrey de Faverches would have known. The present church is of later provenance, erected around the fifteenth century. The inside was gutted by fire in 1961, but fortunately the Seven Sacrament font, together with much fine brass and stone carving, was preserved. There is a magnificent east window telling the story of Walsingham and saints connected with the medieval Priory, and the remodelled interior is full of light, giving a sense of spaciousness and joy.

In the Guild's chapel to the left of the sanctuary where Fr Hope Patten first set up a statue of Our Lady of Walsingham (the one now in the holy house) there is a small replica in memory of earlier times. Mary looks out towards the Priory grounds, her Child on her lap. Here devotion to Our Lady of Walsingham originated in the Anglican Church, and continues to this day.

St Mary's contains some fine contemporary pieces of art by Naomi Blake, Ruth Duckworth and John Riches that are well worth seeing.

The hymn writer and musician George Ratcliffe Woodward ('This joyful Eastertide', 'Ding dong merrily on high') was a former vicar of Walsingham.

The Roman Catholic Church of the Annunciation

The Roman Catholic parish Church of the Annunciation in Friday Market has been newly built to cater for the growing number of pilgrims as well as for a resident parish congregation. Many pilgrimages to the Slipper Chapel begin from here, as it is just next to Elmham House pilgrim accommodation. The present church is built on the site of a former Catholic church that had become too small for its purpose. Note the unusual shape, including a 'Norfolk round tower', and the way it has been constructed to fit naturally into the Norfolk landscape. It was designed by Anthony Rossi, a parishioner, and completed in 2006.

The Orthodox churches

There are two Orthodox churches in the vicinity. One is just up the hill from Friday Market in Station Road, situated in the old railway station house. It is the richly decorated chapel of the Russian Orthodox Brotherhood of St Seraphim. There is an icon workshop on site.

The other Orthodox church is just outside the village, housed in a former Methodist chapel in Great Walsingham. It is dedicated to the Transfiguration.

There is also an Orthodox chapel in the Anglican Shrine Church.

The Methodist Chapel

The Methodist church is in Friday Market next to the Franciscan ruins. Dating from 1793, it is the oldest functioning Methodist chapel in East Anglia. John Wesley is said to have preached at Walsingham when he visited in 1781.

4

Prayers for Pilgrims

Prayers before setting out on a pilgrimage

Psalm 139

V. Our help is in the Name of the Lord.
R. Who made heaven and earth.
V. Watch over all who travel.
R. May your holy angels guard them and keep them safe.

O Lord, you search me and you know me,
you know my resting and my rising,
you discern my purpose from afar.
You mark when I walk or lie down,
all my ways lie open to you.

Response (*R.*): *Lead me, Lord, in the path of life eternal.*

Before ever a word is on my tongue
you know it, O Lord, through and through.
Behind and before you besiege me,
your hand ever laid upon me.
Too wonderful for me is this knowledge,
too high beyond my reach. *R.*

O where can I go from your spirit,
or where can I flee from your face?
If I climb the heavens you are there.
If I lie in the grave you are there. *R.*

If I take the wings of the dawn
and dwell at the sea's furthest end,
even there your hand would lead me,
your right hand would hold me fast. *R.*

If I say, 'Let the darkness hide me
and the light around me be night',
even darkness is not dark for you
and the night is as clear as the day. *R.*

For it was you who created my being,
knit me together in my mother's womb.
I thank you for the wonder of my being,
for the wonders of all your creation. *R.*

Already you knew my soul,
my body held no secret from you
when I was being fashioned in secret
and moulded in the depths of the earth. *R.*

Your eyes saw all my actions,
they were all of them written in your book;
every one of my days was decreed
before one of them came into being. *R.*

To me how mysterious your thoughts,
the sum of them not to be numbered!
If I count them they are more than the sand;
to finish I must be eternal like you. *R.*

O search me, God, and know my heart.
O test me and know my thoughts.
See that I follow not the wrong path
and lead me in the path of life eternal. *R.*

Let us pray

Heavenly Father, protector of those who trust in you, you led your people in safety through the desert and brought them to a land of plenty. Guide us who begin our journey. Fill us with your Spirit of love. Preserve us from all harm and bring us safely to our destination.

May the Lord Jesus be with us to defend us, within us to keep us, before us to lead us, behind us to guard us, above us to bless us. And we ask this through the same Christ our Lord, who lives and reigns with you and the Holy Spirit, God for ever and ever. Amen.

† The Lord bless us and keep us,
the Lord make his face to shine upon us,
the Lord lift up his countenance upon us
and give us peace. Amen.

Prayer before a spiritual pilgrimage

O Jesus, I am a pilgrim on life's road. Be my companion on the way. May I walk with you in ever deeper intimacy, listening to all you have to say to me.

May I journey in spirit, too, with all who are on pilgrimage to Walsingham at this moment, especially those who are laden with a burden of sorrow, pain or suffering. May I carry them in my heart before you with prayer and love.

I think of all the people who have travelled the pilgrim path down the ages, and how Walsingham is saturated with prayer, praise and sacrifice. This way has seen saints and sinners bound together as one in your mystical body, with Mary as their inspiration and model.

Let all who are at the Shrine rediscover a sense of human solidarity and support. Let each care for the other, and let each one know the joy and security of being 'at home' in Mary's Nazareth.

I unite my prayers with those of all pilgrims, offering to you each one with his or her secret joys, sorrows, guilt, fears, sins.

I pray for those struggling with secret sins; those who have ceased to practise their faith because of past hurts; those with marital problems; those who bear a heavy cross without friends to support them and share the burden.

I bring you the whole world, knowing that your cross and your love are more powerful than the powers of darkness. O Jesus, be always our strength and protection. Amen.

Common Prayers

The Sign of the Cross

In the name of the Father and of the Son and of the Holy Spirit. Amen.

The Apostles' Creed

I believe in God, the Father almighty, creator of heaven and earth, and in Jesus Christ, his only Son, our Lord, who was conceived by the Holy Spirit, born of the Virgin Mary, suffered under Pontius Pilate, was crucified, died, and was buried. He descended into hell. The third day he rose again from the dead. He ascended into heaven, and sitteth at the right hand of God the Father almighty. From thence he shall come to judge the living and the dead. I believe in the Holy Spirit, the holy Catholic Church, the Communion of Saints, the forgiveness of sins, the resurrection of the body, and life everlasting. Amen.

Our Father

Our Father, who art in heaven,
hallowed be thy name;
thy kingdom come;
thy will be done on earth as it is in heaven.
Give us this day our daily bread;
and forgive us our trespasses,
as we forgive those who trespass against us;
and lead us not into temptation,
but deliver us from evil.
Amen.

Hail Mary

Hail Mary, full of grace, the Lord is with thee,
blessed art thou among women and blessed is the fruit of
    thy womb, Jesus.
Holy Mary, Mother of God, pray for us sinners,
now and at the hour of our death. Amen.

Glory be to the Father

Glory be to the Father, and to the Son, and to the Holy
    Spirit,
As it was in the beginning, is now and ever shall be, world
    without end. Amen.

The Angelus

V. The angel of the Lord declared unto Mary.
R. And she conceived by the Holy Spirit.

Hail Mary . . .

V. Behold the handmaid of the Lord.
R. Be it done unto me according to thy word.

Hail Mary . . .

V. And the Word was made flesh.
R. And dwelt among us.

Hail Mary ...

V. Pray for us, O holy Mother of God.
R. That we may be made worthy of the promises of Christ.

Let us pray

Pour forth, we beseech thee, O Lord, thy grace into our
  hearts,
that we to whom the incarnation of Christ thy Son was
  made known by the message of an angel,
may by his passion and cross be brought to the glory of his
  resurrection.
Through Christ our Lord, Amen.

Regina Coeli (during the Easter season)

Queen of heaven rejoice. Alleluia!
The Son whom it was your privilege to bear. Alleluia!
Has risen as he said. Alleluia!
Pray to God for us. Alleluia!
Rejoice and be glad, Virgin Mary. Alleluia!
For the Lord has truly risen. Alleluia!

Let us pray

O God, you were pleased to give joy to the world through the
resurrection of your Son, our Lord Jesus Christ. Grant that
through the intercession of the Virgin Mary his mother, we
too may come to possess the joys of life everlasting. Through
the same Christ our Lord. Amen.

The Memorare

Remember, O most gracious Virgin Mary, that never was it
known that anyone who ever fled to your protection, implored

your help or sought your intercession, was left unaided. Inspired by this confidence, I fly to you, O Virgin of virgins, my mother. To you I come, before you I stand, sinful and sorrowful. O Mother of the Word Incarnate, despise not my petitions, but in your mercy hear and answer me. Amen.

A form of morning offering

O Jesus, through the most pure heart of Mary,
I offer you all the prayers, works, sufferings and joys of this
    day,
for all the intentions of your Sacred Heart,
and in union with all the Masses being said throughout the
    whole world. Amen.

Prayers to Our Lady

The Litany of Our Lady of Walsingham

Our Lady of Walsingham, pray to the Lord for us.
Mary conceived without sin, pray to the Lord for us.
Mary the Virgin, pray to the Lord for us.
Mary the Mother of God, pray to the Lord for us.
Mary taken up into Heaven, pray to the Lord for us.
Mary at Bethlehem, pray for all mothers.
Mary at Nazareth, pray for all families.
Mary at Cana, pray for all married couples.
Mary who stood by the cross, pray for all who suffer.
Mary in the upper room, pray for all who wait.
Mary, model of womanhood, pray for all women.

Woman of faith, keep us in mind.
Woman of hope, keep us in mind.
Woman of charity, keep us in mind.
Woman of suffering, keep us in mind.
Woman of anxiety, keep us in mind.
Woman of humility, keep us in mind.
Woman of purity, keep us in mind.
Woman of obedience, keep us in mind.

Woman who wondered, remember us to God.
Woman who listened, remember us to God.
Woman who followed him, remember us to God.
Woman who longed for him, remember us to God.
Woman who loves him, remember us to God.

Mother of God, be our mother always.
Mother of the Church, be our mother always.
Mother of the world, be our mother always.
Mother whom we need, be our mother always.
Mother who went on believing, we thank God for you.
Mother who never lost hope, we thank God for you.
Mother who loved to the end, we thank God for you.

All holy and ever-living God, in giving us Jesus Christ to be our Saviour and Brother, you gave us Mary, his Mother, to be our Mother also; grant, we pray you, that we may be worthy of so great a Brother and so dear a Mother. May we come at last to you, the Father of us all, through Jesus Christ your Son, who lives and reigns with you and the Holy Spirit for ever and ever. Amen.

(From the Litany by the late Father Eric Doyle OFM)

Prayer to Our Lady of Walsingham

O alone of all women, Mother and Virgin
Mother most happy, Virgin most pure,
we, impure as we are, come to you who are all pure.
We greet you, we praise you how we may with our humble
    self-offering.

May your Son grant us that, imitating your holy surrender
we too, by the grace of the Holy Spirit, may deserve to
   conceive the Lord Jesus in our inmost soul
and once conceived, never to lose him. Amen.

Erasmus

O Holy Virgin

O Holy Virgin, in the midst of your days of glory, do not
   forget the sorrows of this earth.
Cast a merciful glance upon those who are struggling
   against difficulties, those who are suffering,
with their lips constantly pressed against life's bitter cup.
Have pity on those who love each other and are separated.
Have pity on our rebellious hearts. Have pity on our weak
   faith.
Have pity on those we love. Have pity on those who weep,
   on those who pray, on those who fear.
Grant hope and peace to all. Amen.

Abbé Perreyve

Almighty Father

Almighty Father of our Lord, Jesus Christ,
you have revealed the beauty of your power by exalting the
   lowly virgin of Nazareth
and making her the mother of our Saviour.
May the prayers of this woman bring Jesus to the waiting
   world
and fill the void of incompletion with the presence of her
   Child.

Missal

A personal fiat prayer

Mary, teach me too to say 'Yes,
I am the handmaid of the Lord.
Let all he wills be done in me.
May his Spirit overshadow me, his love be fruitful in me,
his joy abound in my heart.'
Let there be no 'Yes, but . . .'
which is really a cover for 'No'.
Let it all be 'Yes', plain and simple,
a 'Yes' spoken in trust to the One who is eternally faithful.
 Amen.

O Mary, you are the 'good ground'

O Mary, you are the 'good ground' on which the seed fell.
You have brought forth fruit a hundredfold. Draw us close
to your loving heart and keep us there in gentle lowliness and
perfect trust. Teach us to receive the Spirit as you did; to open
our hearts to the Sacred Word, to ponder it in silence and
yield a rich harvest. Teach us to be apostles of love.

Ruth Burrows

Prayers to the Holy Spirit

Come Holy Spirit

Come Holy Spirit, and send forth from heaven the radiance
 of your light,
Come, Father of the poor, come giver of gifts, come light of
 hearts,

Best Consoler, sweet guest of the soul, sweet refreshment,
In labour rest, coolness in heat, comfort in tears.

O most blessed light, fill the inmost hearts of your faithful;
Without your divine power, nothing is in us except what is
    harmful.
Cleanse what is soiled, water what is dry, heal what is
    wounded;
Bend what is rigid, chafe what is cold, straighten what is
    crooked.
Grant to your faithful who trust in you your sacred seven-
    fold gift,
Grant the reward of virtue, grant at the end salvation, grant
    everlasting joy. Amen.

Prayer of St Mary Magdalen de' Pazzi

Come, Holy Spirit. May the union of the Father and the will
of the Son come to us.

You, Spirit of Truth, are the reward of the saints, the
refreshment of souls, the riches of the poor, the treasury of
lovers, the satisfaction of the hungry, the consolation of the
pilgrim Church. You are the One in whom all treasures are
contained.

Come, you who, descending into Mary, caused the Word
to take flesh; effect in us by grace all you accomplished in her
by grace and by nature.

Come, you who are the nourishment of all chaste thoughts,
the fountain of all mercy, the summit of all purity. Come and
take away from us all that hinders us from being absorbed in
you. Amen.

The secret of sanctity

I am going to reveal to you the secret of sanctity and happiness. Every day, for five minutes, control your imagination
and close your eyes to the things of sense, and your ears to all
the noises of the world, in order to enter into yourself. Then,

in the sanctuary of your baptized soul (which is the temple of the Holy Spirit) speak to that Divine Spirit, saying to him:

'O Holy Spirit, beloved of my soul, I adore you. Enlighten me, guide me, strengthen me, console me, tell me what I should do . . . Give me your orders. I promise to submit myself to all that you desire of me and to accept all that you permit to happen to me. Let me only know your will.'

If you do this, your life will flow along happily, serenely, and full of consolation even in the midst of trials. Grace will be proportioned to the trial, giving you the strength to carry it, and you will arrive at the gate of paradise laden with merit. This submission to the Holy Spirit is the secret of sanctity.

Cardinal Mercier

Prayers before and after Holy Communion

Almighty and ever-living God,

Almighty and ever-living God,
I approach the sacrament of your only-begotten Son,
our Lord Jesus Christ.
I come sick to the doctor of life,
unclean to the fountain of mercy,
blind to the radiance of eternal light,
and poor and needy to the Lord of heaven and earth.
Lord, in your great generosity,
heal my sickness, wash away my defilement,
enlighten my blindness, enrich my poverty,
and clothe my nakedness.
May I receive the bread of angels,
the King of kings and Lord of lords,
with humble reverence,

with purity and faith,
with repentance and love, and the determined purpose
that will help to bring me to salvation.
May I receive the sacrament of the Lord's body and blood,
in its reality and power.
Kind God,
may I receive the body of your only-begotten Son,
our Lord Jesus Christ,
born from the womb of the Virgin Mary,
and so be received into his mystical body,
and numbered among his members.
Loving Father,
as on my earthly pilgrimage
I now receive your beloved Son
under the veil of a sacrament,
may I one day see him face to face in glory,
who lives and reigns with you for ever. Amen.

St Thomas Aquinas

Ave verum

Hail to you, true body sprung
From the Virgin Mary's womb;
The same that on the cross was hung
Bearing for us bitter doom.
You whose side was pierced and flowed
Both with water and with blood;

Grant us of your flesh to taste
When we lie in death's embrace.

O kind, O loving one,
O sweet Jesu, Mary's Son.

Lord Jesus Christ, pierce my soul

Lord Jesus Christ, pierce my soul with your love so that I may always long for you alone, who are the bread of angels and the fulfilment of the soul's deepest desires. May my heart always hunger and feed upon you, so that my soul may be filled with the sweetness of your presence. May my soul thirst for you, who are the source of life, wisdom, knowledge, light and all the riches of God our Father. May I always seek and find you, think upon you, speak to you and do all things for the honour and glory of your holy name. Be always my only hope, my peace, my refuge and my help in whom my heart is rooted, so that I may never be separated from you.

St Bonaventure

Anima Christi

Soul of Christ, sanctify me,
Body of Christ, save me
Blood of Christ, inebriate me
Water from the side of Christ, wash me,
Passion of Christ, strengthen me.
O good Jesus, hear me,
Within your wounds hide me,
Let me not be separated from you.
From the malicious enemy defend me.
In the hour of my death call me
And bid me come to you,
That with your saints I may praise you
For ever and ever. Amen.

Act of spiritual communion (when unable to receive the sacrament)

My Jesus, I believe that you are truly present in the most Blessed Sacrament. I love you above all things, and I desire to possess you within my soul. Since I am unable now to receive you sacramentally, come at least spiritually into my heart. I embrace you as if you were already there, and I unite myself wholly to you; never permit me to be separated from you.

St Alphonsus

Prayers for various occasions

The divine praises

Blessed be God.
Blessed be his holy Name.
Blessed be Jesus Christ, true God and true Man.
Blessed be the Name of Jesus.
Blessed be his most Sacred Heart.
Blessed be his most Precious Blood.
Blessed be Jesus in the Most Holy Sacrament of the Altar.
Blessed be the Holy Spirit the Paraclete.
Blessed be the great Mother of God, Mary most holy.
Blessed be her holy and immaculate Conception.
Blessed be her glorious Assumption.
Blessed be the name of Mary, Virgin and Mother.
Blessed be St Joseph, her spouse most chaste.
Blessed be God in his Angels and in his Saints.

Prayer before a crucifix

Behold, O kind and most sweet Jesus, I cast myself on my knees in your sight, and with the most fervent desire of my soul I pray and beseech you that you would impress upon my heart lively sentiments of faith, hope and charity, with a true repentance for my sins and a firm desire of amendment. While with deep affection and grief of soul I ponder within myself and mentally contemplate your five most precious wounds, having before my eyes that which David spoke in prophecy of you, O good Jesus: 'They pierced my hands and my feet; they have numbered all my bones.'

Acts of faith, hope and love

Lord, I believe in you: increase my faith.
I trust in you: strengthen my trust.
I love you: let me love you more and more.
I am sorry for my sins: deepen my sorrow.

I worship you as my first beginning,
I long for you as my last end,
I praise you as my constant helper,
and call on you as my loving protector.

Guide me by your wisdom,
correct me with your justice,
comfort me with your mercy,
protect me with your power.

I offer you, Lord, my thoughts: to be fixed on you;
my words: to have you for their theme;
my actions: to reflect my love for you;
my sufferings: to be endured for your greater glory.

I want to do what you ask of me:
in the way you ask
for as long as you ask,
because you ask it.

Lord, enlighten my understanding,
strengthen my will,
purify my heart,
and make me holy.

Hymn of the holy name of Jesus

O Jesus, it is sweet to remember you, true joy of the heart;
but sweeter than honey, sweeter than anything, is your
    presence.
It is the most delightful song, joyful to hear,
it is the sweetest thought, Jesus, Son of God.
You are the hope of the repentant, loving with the one who
    asks,
good to the one who seeks.
So how could one describe what it means to find you?
No spoken word can describe, no written word express,
only the one who has experienced it can believe
what it is to love Jesus.
O Jesus, be our joy, and one day be our eternal rest.
To you be the glory, now and for ever. Amen.

Prayer of St Richard of Chichester

Thanks be to you my Lord Jesus Christ,
for all the blessings which you have given to me,
all the sufferings you have borne for me.
O most merciful Friend, Brother and Redeemer,
may I know you more clearly, love you more dearly, follow
    you more nearly,
day by day. Amen.

Meditation on providence

My God, you have created me to do some definite service.
You have given some definite work to me which has been
    given to no other.
I have my place in your plan.
I may never know what it is in this life but I will be told it in
    the next.
Therefore I will trust you in all things.
If I am sick, my sickness may serve you.
If I am worried, my worry may serve you.

If I am in sorrow, my sorrow may serve you.
You do nothing in vain, you know what you are doing.
You may take away my friends, you may put me among
    strangers,
You may make me feel forgotten; you may make my spirits
    sink.
You may hide my future from me.
Still you know what you are doing and I trust you. Amen.

Cardinal Newman

Prayer of St Francis

Lord, make me an instrument of your peace.
Where there is hatred, let me sow love;
where there is injury, pardon;
where there is doubt, faith;
where there is despair, hope;
where there is darkness, light;
where there is sadness, joy.
O divine Master, grant that I may not so much seek
to be consoled as to console,
to be understood as to understand,
to be loved as to love.
For it is in giving that we receive,
it is in pardoning that we are pardoned,
and in dying that we are born to eternal life. Amen.

Fill us with your love

Fill us with your love in the morning
and we will live the whole day in joy and praise.
    Lord listen to us.

Let my prayer rise before you like incense,
and my hands like the evening offering.
    Lord listen to us.

Restore sight to the blind;
straighten those who are bent.
>> *Lord listen to us.*

Protect the weak and the needy;
support the widow and the orphan.
>> *Lord listen to us.*

Come and cure all broken hearts;
give justice to the oppressed.
>> *Lord listen to us.*

Give bread to the hungry;
give freedom to prisoners.
>> *Lord listen to us.*

May your eternal kingdom be ours;
give salvation to those who love you.
>> *Lord listen to us.*

Based on Pss. 90.14; 141.2; 146.7–9

God be in my head

God be in my head and in my understanding.
God be in mine eyes and in my looking.
God be in my mouth and in my speaking.
God be in my heart and in my thinking.
God be at my end and at my departing.

O Life, giving life to all!

O Life, giving life to all! Do not deny me that living water
which you promised to all who longed for it. I thirst for it,
Lord, I long for it, I come to you.

St Teresa of Avila

God, of your goodness

God, of your goodness give me yourself, for you are enough
  for me.
I cannot ask anything less to be worthy of you.
If I were to ask less I should always be in want.
Only in you have I all.

Julian of Norwich

Dearest Jesus, help me

Dearest Jesus, help me to spread your fragrance everywhere
  I go.
Flood my soul with your spirit and life,
penetrate and possess my whole being so utterly
that all my life may be but a radiance of yours.
Shine through me, and be so in me, that everyone I come in
  contact with
may feel your presence in my soul.
May they look up and see no longer me, but only Jesus.
Amen.

Cardinal Newman

Renewal of baptismal promises

Today I freely renew the promises of my baptism, asking
that I may be clothed in the garments of Christlikeness and
that Jesus alone may be the Lord of my heart. As I take this
blessed water I ask to be cleansed of all my sins and to be
renewed in grace as a child of God.

I believe in all that the Christian faith teaches, I hope in the
promise of eternal life and I desire to grow daily in the love
of God and others.

May Christ form his own image in me, and may my baptism
come to completion in a life filled with the Spirit, a witness
to others that Jesus brings healing, forgiveness and joy into
our broken world.

Mary, my mother, form the image of Jesus within me and make me all his own.

My patron saints, whose name I received at my baptism, pray for me.

Our Father, may everything I do

Our Father, may everything I do begin with your
    inspiration, continue with your help,
and reach perfection under your guidance.
With your loving care guide all my daily actions.
Help me to persevere with love and sincerity.
Teach me to judge wisely of the things of earth and to love
    the things of heaven.
Keep me in your presence and never let me be separated
    from you.
Your Spirit made me your child, confident to call you Father;
Make your love the foundation of my life.
And I ask this through Jesus your beloved Son. Amen.

Love of the Heart of Jesus

Love of the Heart of Jesus, inflame my heart.
Charity of the Heart of Jesus, flow into my heart.
Strength of the Heart of Jesus, support my heart.
Mercy of the Heart of Jesus, pardon my heart.
Patience of the Heart of Jesus, grow not weary of my heart
Kingdom of the Heart of Jesus, be in my heart.
Wisdom of the Heart of Jesus, teach my heart.
Will of the Heart of Jesus, guide my heart.
Zeal of the Heart of Jesus, consume my heart.
Immaculate Virgin Mary, pray for me to the Heart of Jesus.

Lord Jesus Christ, you said to your apostles

Lord Jesus Christ, you said to your apostles: 'I leave you
    peace, my peace I give you.'
Look not on our sins, but on the faith of your Church,
and grant us the peace and unity of your kingdom where
you live for ever and ever. Amen.

Missal

Jesus alone for my goal

Jesus alone for my Goal,
Jesus alone for my Master,
Jesus alone for my Model,
Jesus alone for Guide,
Jesus alone for Joy and Riches,
Jesus alone for my Friend.

St Bernadette

O sweetest love of God

O sweetest love of God too little known, whoever finds you is
at rest; let everything change, O my God, that we may rest in
you. O my God, how sweet your presence is to me, you who
are the one true Good. I will rejoice in nothing until I am in
your arms. O Lord, I beseech you, leave me not for a moment,
because I know not the value of my soul. Amen.

St John of the Cross

A prayer of St Ambrose

Lord, teach me to seek you, and reveal yourself to me when
    I seek you.
For I cannot seek you unless you teach me,
nor find you except you reveal yourself.
Let me seek you in longing, let me long for you in seeking.
Let me find you in love, and love you in finding you. Amen.

Set me, Father, in the full radiance

Set me, Father, in the full radiance of the face of your Son
that I may catch his beauty, and by what I become
show all the world that Jesus is still living in his Church.
   Amen.

Heart of Jesus, think on me

Heart of Jesus, think on me.
Eyes of Jesus, look on me.
Face of Jesus, shine on me.
Hands of Jesus, bless me.
Feet of Jesus, guide me.
Arms of Jesus, hold me.
Body of Jesus, feed me.
Blood of Jesus, cleanse me
Make me, Jesus, your own, here and in the world to come.
   Amen.

The Jesus prayer

Lord Jesus Christ, Son of God,
have mercy on me, a sinner.

For others

Hear me, Lord, on behalf of those who are dear to me,
all whom I have in mind at this moment.
Be near them in all their anxieties and all their worries.
Give them the help of your saving grace.
I commend them all with trustful confidence to your
   merciful love.
Remember, Lord, all who are mindful of me, all who have
   asked me to pray for them,
all who have been kind to me,
all whom I have wronged by ill will or misunderstanding.

Give us all grace to bear each other's faults and to share
each other's burdens.

Have mercy on the souls of our loved ones who have gone
before us.

Grant them eternal peace and happiness with you. Amen.

Saint Teresa's bookmark

Let nothing disturb you,
Let nothing affright you,
All things pass away;
God alone abideth.
Patience obtains all things.
Whoever has God
Can want for nothing.
God alone sufficeth.

St Teresa of Avila

Canticle of the creatures

All-Highest omnipotent, good Lord, to you be praise, glory
and honour and every blessing.

To you alone they are due, and no one is worthy to speak
your name.

Be praised my Lord for all creatures, especially Brother Sun,
who makes daytime,

and through him you give us light. He is beautiful, radiant
with great splendour,

and he is a sign that tells, All-Highest, of you.

Be praised my Lord for Sister Moon and the stars,

You formed them in the sky, bright and precious and
beautiful.

Be praised my Lord for Brother Wind, and for the air and
the clouds,

and for fair and every kind of weather by which you give
your creatures food.

Be praised my Lord for Sister Water, who is most humble
and useful, lovely and chaste.

Be praised my Lord for Brother Fire, through whom you
  light up the night for us,
and he is beautiful and jolly, lusty and strong.
Be praised my Lord for our sister, Mother Earth, who keeps
  us and feeds us,
and brings forth fruits of many kinds, with coloured flowers
  and plants as well.
Be praised my Lord for those who grant pardon for love of
  you and bear with sickness and vexation.
Blessed are those who bear these things peaceably because
  by you, All-Highest, they will be crowned.
Be praised my Lord for our sister Death, whom no living
  person can escape.
Woe to those who die in mortal sin. Blessed are those whom
  she will find doing your holy will,
for to them the second death will do no harm.
Bless and praise my Lord, thank him and serve him in all
  humility.

St Francis of Assisi

Prayer of abandonment

Father,
I abandon myself into your hands,
do with me what you will.
Whatever you may do, I thank you;
I am ready for all, I accept all.
Let only your will be done in me
and in all your creatures.
I wish no more than this, O Lord.
Into your hands I commend my soul;
I offer it to you with all the love of my heart
for I love you Lord,
and so need to give myself,
to surrender myself into your hands without reserve
and with boundless confidence,
for you are my Father.

Charles de Foucauld

Prayer to accept suffering when it comes

My great God, you have humbled yourself and have been lifted up on the tree! Though I am not fit to ask you for suffering as a gift, at least I will beg of you grace to meet suffering well, when you in your love and wisdom bring it upon me.

Let me bear pain, reproach, disappointment, slander, anxiety, suspense, when it comes. I wish to bear insults meekly and to return good for evil. I wish to humble myself in all things and to be silent when I am ill used, and to be patient when sorrow or pain are prolonged. And all for the love of you and your cross, knowing that in this way I shall gain the promise of this life and of the next. Amen.

Cardinal Newman

Prayer for missionaries

O God, bless all those who have gone out to bring the message of the gospel to other lands.

We place before you especially: those who have had to leave their families behind; those who have to struggle with a new language and with new ways of thought; those who face constant discouragement in situations in which no progress ever seems to be made.

Bless all those who preach in the villages, the towns and the cities.

Bless those who teach in schools and colleges.

Bless those who work in hospitals and among the sick.

Bless those who have laid their gifts of craftsmanship or administration on the altar of missionary service.

Help us at home never to forget them and always to pray for them.

And bring quickly the day when the knowledge of you will cover the earth as the waters cover the sea.

We pray this in the name of Jesus, who is Lord. Amen.

Society of Mill Hill Missionaries

A prayer for priests

Lord Jesus, you have chosen your priests from among us and sent them out to proclaim your word and to act in your name. For so great a gift to your Church we give you praise and thanksgiving. We ask you to fill them with the fire of your love, that their ministry may reveal your presence in the Church. Since they are earthen vessels, we pray that your power may shine out through their weakness. In their afflictions let them never be crushed; in their doubts never despair; in temptation never be destroyed; in persecution never abandoned. Inspire them through prayer to live each day the mystery of your dying and rising. In times of weakness send them your Spirit, and help them to praise your heavenly Father and to pray for poor sinners. By the same Holy Spirit put your word on their lips and your love in their hearts, to bring good news to the poor and healing to the broken-hearted. And may the gift of Mary your mother to the disciple you loved, be your gift to every priest. Grant that she who formed you in your human image may form them in your divine image, by the power of your Spirit, to the glory of God the Father. Amen.

Prayer in honour of St Joseph

God our Father, in every age you call men and women to develop and use their gifts for the good of others. With St Joseph as our example and guide, help us to do the work you have given us. Help those who are unemployed to use their talents in your service and to find work. May we all come to the rewards you have promised. We ask this through Christ our Lord. Amen.

Prayer in honour of St Thérèse

Eternal Father, whose infinite love watches in wisdom over each day of my life; grant me the light to see in sorrow as in joy, in trial as in peace, in uncertainty as in confidence, the way your divine providence has marked for me. Give me that faith and trust in your care for me which was so pleasing to you in St Thérèse of the Child Jesus, and I will walk in darkness as in light, holding your hand and finding in all the blessings I receive from your loving bounty that everything is a grace. Amen.

Night prayer

Watch, dear Lord, with those who wake or watch or weep
  tonight,
and give your angels charge over those who sleep.
Tend your sick ones, O Lord Christ,
rest your weary ones, bless your dying ones,
soothe your suffering ones, shield your joyous ones,
and all for your love's sake. Amen.

St Augustine

The Sacrament of Reconciliation

In the Sacrament of Reconciliation we proclaim our sinfulness before God and celebrate the joy of forgiveness. This sacrament should be a source of great peace and happiness for us, because our faith assures us of the forgiveness of sins through the passion, death and resurrection of Jesus Christ our Lord.

Before going into the confessional or the reconciliation room, spend time quietly pondering, reflecting on your life. Ask the Lord to show you where you fail most and what you have done wrong. Realize that you are bringing yourself before a loving and forgiving God who is waiting to receive you and welcome you home.

Some of the following biblical passages may help you to prepare your mind and heart:

'Wash me from my guilt and cleanse me from my sin.'
Ps. 51

'Though your sins are like scarlet they shall be white as snow.'
Isa. 1.16–18

'I will heal their faithlessness and love them freely.'
Hos. 14.4–7

'Have courage, your sins are forgiven,' Jesus says to the paralytic.
Matt. 9.1–8

Jesus eats with tax collectors and sinners. He has not come to call the righteous but sinners.
Matt. 9.9–13

Jesus calls to himself all who are weighed down by heavy burdens.
Matt. 11.25–30

The sinful woman anoints Jesus. All her sins are forgiven because she has loved so much.
Luke 7.36–50

Jesus goes after the lost sheep and rejoices when he finds it.
Luke 15.1–7

The father welcomes home the prodigal son and prepares a feast for him.
Luke 15.11–32

Jesus forgives even the men who are crucifying him.
Luke 23.32–34

Jesus gives his apostles power to forgive sins and to proclaim his peace.
John 20.19–23

When you go in to the priest, kneel or sit as you wish. The priest will say a few words of welcome or read a short passage from the Bible. Then tell your sins in a simple and straightforward way, mentioning especially any serious wrongs you may have done. After you have finished the priest may give you some encouragement or advice and tell you to say some prayers as a form of penance. Then he will invite you to make an act of sorrow. You can do this in your own words or in the words of one of the following prayers:

Lord Jesus Christ, you chose to be called the friend of sinners. By your saving death and resurrection free me from my sins and from every evil. May your peace take root in my heart and bring forth a harvest of love, holiness and truth. Amen.

Heavenly Father, Jesus told us how lovingly you welcome home the sinful child who returns to you. I come before you with sorrow. Purify my heart and give me the grace to live the new life of Easter, ever confident in your saving power. Amen.

Lord Jesus, you are the Lamb of God who takes away the sins of the world. Cleanse my soul of all sin, renew in me the grace of my baptism and help me to live in peace with all. Amen.

Lord Jesus Christ, look not on my sins but on the faith of your Church. Create a clean heart within me, and in your goodness lead me along the path of light. Amen.

Heavenly Father, I believe in your mercy and forgiveness. Heal my soul, for I have sinned against you. I ask this through Christ our Lord. Amen.

After you have made an act of sorrow the priest will pronounce over you the forgiveness of God in these words:

God the Father of mercies,
through the death and resurrection of his Son,
has reconciled the world to himself
and sent the Holy Spirit among us for the forgiveness of sins.
Through the ministry of the Church
may God give you pardon and peace,
and I absolve you from your sins
† in the name of the Father, and of the Son, and of the Holy
    Spirit. Amen.
  The Lord has freed you from your sins. Go in the peace of
    Christ. Amen.

When you leave the confessional kneel down and say your penance. Then spend some time in quiet prayer, praising God for his goodness in giving us this wonderful sacrament.

Vespers of Our Lady of Walsingham

V. O God, come to our aid.
R. O Lord, make haste to help us. Glory be . . .

Hymn

The angel Gabriel from heaven came,
his wings as drifted snow, his eyes as flame.
'All hail,' said he, 'thou lowly maiden Mary,
most highly favoured lady.' *Gloria.*

'For now a blessed mother thou shalt be,
all generations laud and honour thee.
Thy Son shall be Emmanuel, by seers foretold,
most highly favoured lady.' *Gloria.*

Then gentle Mary meekly bowed her head,
'To me be as it pleases God,' she said.
'My soul shall laud and magnify his holy name.'
Most highly favoured lady. *Gloria.*

Antiphon

Do not be afraid, Mary, for you have found favour with God.
Behold, you will conceive and bear a son, and he will be
called the Son of the Most High.

Psalm 121

I rejoiced when I heard them say,
'Let us go to God's house.'
And now our feet are standing
within your gates, O Jerusalem.

Jerusalem is built as a city
strongly compact.
It is there that the tribes go up,
the tribes of the Lord.

For Israel's law it is
there to praise the Lord's name.
There were set the thrones of judgement
of the house of David.

For the peace of Jerusalem pray:
'Peace be to your homes!
May peace reign in your walls,
in your palaces, peace!'

For love of my brethren and friends
I say: 'Peace upon you!'
For love of the house of the Lord
I will ask for your good.
Glory be . . .

Antiphon

Do not be afraid, Mary, for you have found favour with God.
Behold, you will conceive and bear a son, and he will be
called the Son of the Most High.

Antiphon

I am the servant of the Lord; let it be as you have said.

Psalm 131

O Lord, my heart is not proud,
nor haughty my eyes.
I have not gone after things too great,
nor marvels beyond me.

Truly I have set my soul
in silence and peace;
as a child has rest in its mother's arms,
even so is my soul.

O Israel, hope in the Lord,
both now and for ever.
Glory be . . .

Antiphon

I am the servant of the Lord; let it be as you have said.

Antiphon

The Word of God, born of the Father before time began,
humbled himself for love of us, and became man.

Philippians 2.6–11

Though he was in the form of God,
Jesus did not count equality with God a thing to be grasped.

He emptied himself, taking the form of a servant,
being born in human likeness.

And being found in human form,
he humbled himself and became obedient unto death,
even death on a cross.

Therefore God has highly exalted him,
and bestowed on him the name which is above every name,

that at the name of Jesus every knee should bow,
in heaven and on earth and under the earth,

and every tongue confess that Jesus Christ is Lord,
to the glory of God the Father.
Glory be . . .

Antiphon

The Word of God, born of the Father before time began, humbled himself for love of us, and became man.

Scripture

Sing aloud, O daughter of Sion, shout O Israel!
Rejoice and exult with all your heart, O daughter of
    Jerusalem!
The King of Israel, the Lord, is in your midst; you shall fear
    evil no more.
He will rejoice over you with gladness, he will renew you in
    his love.

Responsary

Hail Mary, full of grace, the Lord is with you.
Response (R): Hail Mary full of grace, the Lord is with you.
Blessed are you among women, and blest the fruit of your
    womb. *R.*
Glory be to the Father and to the Son and to the Holy Spirit.
    R.

Magnificat

(Tune: 'Amazing Grace')

My soul proclaims the Lord my God,
my spirit sings his praise.
He looks on me, he lifts me up,
and gladness fills my days.

All nations now will share my joy;
his gifts he has outpoured.
His little one he has made great;
I magnify the Lord.

His mercy is for evermore;
his holy name I praise.
His strong right arm puts down the proud;
the lowly he does raise.

He fills the hungry with good things;
the rich he sends away.
The promise made to Abraham
is fulfilled by him each day.

To Father, Son and Spirit blessed,
the God whom we adore,
be glory, as it was, is now,
and shall be evermore.

Intercessions

The response (R.) is: 'Lord, fill us with your grace.'

Eternal Father, through your angel you made known your
salvation to Mary. Full of confidence, we earnestly pray. R.

By the consent of your handmaid and the power of the Holy
Spirit, your Word came to dwell among us. Open our hearts
to receive Christ as Mary the Virgin received him. R.

You look with compassion on the lowly and fill the starving with good things. Encourage the downhearted, help all those in need and comfort those near to death. *R.*

You called Mary to be mother in the house of Jesus and Joseph. Through her prayers help all mothers to make their homes places of love and holiness. *R.*

Mary was your faithful handmaid who treasured your words in her heart. Through her intercession let us become devoted disciples of Jesus your Son. *R.*

Let the dead enter with joy into your presence, to rejoice with Mary and all the saints before you. *R.*

Let us join our prayers with Mary as we pray in the words which her Son gave us: *Our Father . . .*

Let us pray

Lord, open our hearts to your grace.
Through the angel's message to Mary
we have learned to believe in the incarnation of Christ your
    Son;
lead us by his passion and cross to the glory of his
    resurrection.
We make our prayer through our Lord Jesus Christ your
    Son,
who lives and reigns with you in the unity of the Holy Spirit,
one God for ever and ever. Amen

The Stations of the Cross

In making the Stations of the Cross we walk in spirit with Jesus to Calvary, remembering all that he has suffered on our behalf. At the same time we pray for all who, at this moment, are sharing in some way in the redemption of the world through their own suffering. One day with Jesus, we and they will know the joy of resurrection if we persevere to the end.

There are outdoor Stations of the Cross in the grounds of both shrines as well as in the churches.

Opening prayer

Jesus, I am about to make the Way of the Cross. Be with me, and help me to understand the love with which you suffered; a love you want to share with me now as I walk with you to Calvary. Amen.

1 Jesus is condemned to death

Jesus stands before Pilate bound and humiliated. A robber has been preferred before him because the leaders are jealous of Jesus' freedom and goodness. His way of living has shown them up for the mean-spirited people they are.

For his part, Pilate has been cowardly in condemning a man he knows to be innocent. He is more interested in saving his own skin than in saving Jesus, a helpless prisoner.

It isn't always easy to take responsibility for my decisions and choices, and act according to my conscience. It may mean going against the crowd and that takes courage. Or I can judge and condemn others because they touch something in me that I don't want to look at: my jealousy, my fear, my desire for respectability at all costs.

Prayer: *Jesus, help me to stand with you in truth and be*

ready to take the consequences of being a person of integrity.
Amen.

2 Jesus accepts the cross

Jesus takes the cross that is laid upon him. It isn't something he has chosen. It is something given; something he would no doubt have rather been without, but for our sake he accepts it with love.

Life brings its crosses to each of us. I do not choose my suffering, rather it is chosen for me, given to me. What makes a difference is how I accept it. If I do so grudgingly, if I grumble and complain, I only make things worse.

But if, like Jesus, I accept with love the painful and difficult things of life as being laid on me by a loving Father, then I shall discover that these will take me, not just to Calvary, but to the joy of the resurrection.

Prayer: *Jesus, help me to put as much love as possible into the difficulties of life. May I shoulder my cross with you beside me. With you may I understand that love makes all burdens light. Amen.*

3 Jesus falls the first time

Jesus does not march off to Calvary like some strong superman. He goes as one who is weak, one who stumbles and falls. What a consolation for us when we see that Jesus is fully human! He has to get up and go on even though the way is painful, even though he finds himself down in the dust.

I often fall; but then I am tempted to stay down and complain, or say it's no use trying any more.

I don't like to look foolish, someone who doesn't succeed at first go. But neither did Jesus.

The only difference is that I don't get up and go on as he did, relying on the Father to give me strength.

Prayer: *Jesus, never let me give up, no matter how often I fall. Keep my eyes on the goal and help me to go forward with you beside me. Amen.*

4 Jesus meets his mother

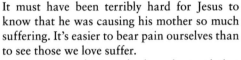

It must have been terribly hard for Jesus to know that he was causing his mother so much suffering. It's easier to bear pain ourselves than to see those we love suffer.

But Jesus and Mary both understand that this is part of God's plan for them and for the world.

So many mothers, members of families and close friends are in anguish in many places even today, because they are separated from those they love by war, prison, persecution or exile.

Mary can be for them, and for us, the model of someone who selflessly allows a loved one to embrace their own destiny, and offers silent, strong support without any self-pity.

Prayer: *Jesus and Mary, show me how to bear suffering with and for others, not thinking of myself but of them. Amen.*

5 Jesus is helped by Simon of Cyrene

Scripture tells of how a passer-by, Simon of Cyrene, was forced to help Jesus carry the Cross. Jesus was so weak from sleeplessness and loss of blood that his captors were afraid he would not reach Calvary alive.

No doubt Simon felt put upon. It was Passover time and he was on holiday, yet he had to shoulder the cross of a condemned criminal. Only later he must have realized that this was not his moment of shame but his moment of glory, the only incident in his life which would make him remembered.

Do I help others who suffer, or am I too busy grumbling about my own lot in life? If I do help, it is truly Jesus himself whom I relieve of his burden.

Prayer: *Jesus, help me to recognize you in those who suffer and be always ready to lend a hand cheerfully. Amen.*

6 Veronica wipes the face of Jesus

It is only legend which says that a woman came forward to wipe the face of Jesus as he stumbled on, and then found his face impressed on the linen she had used. Tradition then gave her the name of Veronica – that is, *vera icon* or 'true image'.

Many people are mocked, taunted or despised because of their race, colour or religion. In many cases we avoid those who are different from ourselves. We don't want to get involved, like the crowd who just stood and watched Jesus go to Calvary. Only one person had the courage to do an act of kindness on her own initiative.

Am I like Veronica when it comes to showing sympathy for those who are marginalized? If so, then Jesus will imprint his image on my own heart.

Prayer: *Jesus, you said that what is done to the least person is done to you. Give me the courage to reach out and help all who need it. Then I too will become a bearer of your image on earth. Amen.*

7 Jesus falls a second time

Another fall. What a humiliation! Jesus finds himself down in the mud and dust once again. He certainly doesn't look clean and heroic; he is weary, dirty, jeered at by the onlookers.

Even though Simon has relieved Jesus of some of the weight, he is still unable to cope.

How hard it can be for me to accept my weaknesses patiently when it seems that others are laughing at my failures.

Jesus can show me how to turn my falls into steps that take me on to victory if only I continue in his company, relying not on myself but on him, who knows what it is to be seen as a failure.

Prayer: *Jesus, show me how to make the most of my falls by learning from them to rely on your grace and not on my own strength. Amen.*

8 The women of Jerusalem mourn for Jesus

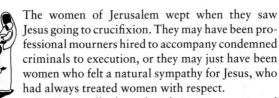

The women of Jerusalem wept when they saw Jesus going to crucifixion. They may have been professional mourners hired to accompany condemned criminals to execution, or they may just have been women who felt a natural sympathy for Jesus, who had always treated women with respect.

But Jesus tells them that their tears are wasted on him. It is they and their children who will suffer more when, in the future, Jerusalem will be put to the sword.

It isn't easy to see clearly enough to weep for the right things. I can weep uselessly for Jesus who died long ago, and yet I don't see that I am asked instead to comfort a bereaved neighbour, a refugee who is a stranger in my town, an elderly person who longs for a visit.

Prayer: *Jesus, help me to see where sympathy is really needed and offer it willingly. Amen.*

9 Jesus falls a third time

Another fall. Jesus is utterly exhausted as he approaches Calvary. He wonders if he will ever get there alive. Yet he knows he must, and so he forces himself to continue.

It's like trying to cope with a fault of my own such as impatience, meanness, bad temper. I fall, I fall again . . . and again . . . I make up my mind that I won't fall again; but I do, countless times. No remedy seems to work!

But that is the moment when I can rely on Jesus to help me not to give up in despair. He knows what it is to be weak and needy. He knows too that in the end there is victory if I persevere. Trying, not succeeding, makes the difference.

Prayer: *Jesus, however hard my own path seems, may I trust you to see me through to the end. Amen.*

10 Jesus is stripped of his garments

Jesus is shamed by being stripped in front of everyone before being nailed to the cross.

Clothes give us a sense of dignity, but nakedness is considered shameful. That is why unjust regimes often strip prisoners before interrogation and torture. It makes them feel exposed and vulnerable.

On the other hand, sick people have to be helped by others to perform the most private bodily functions.

Jesus accepts being naked because he has absolutely nothing to hide. His dignity doesn't consist in fine clothes or being nicely dressed. It consists in his status as a child of God, who is loved just as he is, without any disguise.

Prayer: *Jesus, help me to give others a proper respect at all times rather than judging by outward appearances. Amen.*

11 Jesus is nailed to the cross

Jesus must have experienced terrible agony when the nails were driven through his flesh, pinning his body to the cross. No longer could he move by himself; he had only to wait now for death to come as he hung helpless and in pain.

I too am nailed to the cross of my life by things I cannot help or change: illness, temperamental difficulties, lack of talent, traumas suffered in childhood which have left a permanent mark, personal sin.

Or maybe I have chosen a way of life that deprives me of personal freedom because I must serve and help others. I am nailed by circumstances and cannot move. Whatever the case, I can be sure that Jesus is with me and with all who suffer.

Prayer: *Jesus, you were nailed to the cross and held there by love. May I love what holds me on my cross with you. Amen.*

12 Jesus dies on the cross

We all have to die at some time, but Jesus dies when he is still young. He dies unjustly, by violence. Yet he forgives those who have tormented him and condemned him. He promises paradise to the robber crucified with him. He remembers his mother who stands by the cross, and confides her to the care of the apostle John. Jesus doesn't leave any loose ends behind him, so he is able to say at the last, 'All is finished. Father, I place my soul in your loving hands.'

Let us pray for all who are dying today, especially those who die young, those who die suddenly through war or violence, those who die unloved or uncared for.

And may I too be ready for my own death when it comes.

Prayer: *Holy Mary, Mother of God, pray for us sinners now and at the hour or our death. Amen.*

13 Jesus is taken down from the cross

When he is dead, Jesus is taken down from the cross and laid in his mother's arms. Can we even imagine what it must have been like for Mary to hold her dead son after seeing him die in agony?

But Mary understands, even in her sorrow, that Jesus has accomplished the Father's will, so beneath her tears she is at peace.

It isn't easy to accept that loved ones must die.

It isn't easy to see why or to what purpose they have been taken from us. All we can do is believe in faith that 'All shall be well, and all shall be well, and all manner of things shall be well' (Julian of Norwich).

We cannot see into God's designs. All we know is that he never deserts anyone, no matter what.

Prayer: *Father help me to trust even in sorrow, believing that you have a plan for each one, just as you had a plan for your own Son. Amen.*

14 Jesus is laid in the tomb

All is silent now. Jesus is buried as his friends mourn. The stone is rolled in front of the tomb. It seems as if everything is over for ever. A beautiful and compassionate person has been killed, his life ended.

Death always seems so final.

But we know that this is not really the end. God the Father will raise Jesus to life because his was a life of total love – and love endures for ever.

What seems like failure is really victory. Jesus has conquered death for ever.

Right now Jesus is silent, dead, buried; but inwardly life and love are ready to burst forth eternally.

Can I too trust that, in all the little deaths of my life, God is awaiting the moment to bring forth something new and better, if only I give him time?

Prayer: *Lord, I believe. Help my unbelief. Amen.*

15 The resurrection

Jesus is risen. Alleluia!
Jesus is alive. Alleluia!
Jesus brings joy.
Jesus brings peace.

He asks us not to be afraid, to touch his wounds and know that he now lives for ever.

In him we too have life, peace, joy. These are his gifts to us. We have only to ask for them.

Prayer: *Lord Jesus Christ, by your saving death and resurrection free me from every sin and all evil. May your peace take root in my heart and bring forth a harvest of love, holiness, joy and truth. Amen.*

The Rosary of Our Lady

The rosary is a very old prayer by which we contemplate the life of Jesus through the eyes of his mother; for this we use special beads, and as the beads pass through our fingers we spend time thinking on the mystery before us. There are five Joyful Mysteries: the annunciation, the visitation, the nativity, the presentation in the temple and the finding of Jesus in the temple. The five Sorrowful Mysteries are: the agony in the garden, the scourging, the crowning with thorns, the carrying of the cross and the crucifixion of Jesus. The five Glorious Mysteries are: the resurrection, the ascension, the descent of the Holy

Spirit at Pentecost, the Assumption of our Blessed Lady and her crowning in heaven.

The rosary is made up of 'decades'. A decade is one 'Our Father' followed by ten 'Hail Marys' and a 'Glory be'. It is usual to say five decades at a time, either the Joyful, Sorrowful or Glorious Mysteries.

Begin with the sign of the cross. Pray the Apostles' Creed holding the crucifix and continue on the straight piece of the rosary with one 'Our Father', three 'Hail Marys' and a 'Glory be'. Then to start the first decade pray one 'Our Father', continue with ten 'Hail Marys', and end with a 'Glory be'. Each decade gives you time to think on one of the mysteries as you pray the 'Hail Marys'. When you have completed five decades, end with the 'Hail, Holy Queen' and any other prayers you may wish to add.

Hail, Holy Queen

Hail, holy queen, Mother of mercy; hail, our life, our sweetness, and our hope; to thee do we cry, poor banished children of Eve; to thee do we send up our sighs, mourning and weeping in this valley of tears. Turn then, most gracious advocate, thine eyes of mercy towards us; and after this our exile, show unto us the blessed fruit of thy womb, Jesus, O clement, O loving, O sweet Virgin Mary.

V. Queen of the most holy rosary, pray for us.
R. That we may be made worthy of the promises of Christ.

Let us pray

O God, whose only-begotten Son, by his life, death and resurrection has purchased for us the rewards of eternal life; grant, we beseech you, that meditating upon the mysteries in the most holy rosary of the Blessed Virgin Mary, we may both imitate what they contain and obtain what they promise, through the same Christ our Lord. Amen.

The Joyful Mysteries

1 The annunciation

Consider how Mary says 'Yes' to conceiving Jesus in her womb. Ask for the grace to say your own 'Yes' to bringing Jesus into the world through your own life.

2 The visitation

Consider Mary visiting her cousin Elizabeth and the joy the two women share in praising God for all his mercies. Ask for the grace to take Jesus with you to all the people you meet this day, and for a spirit of gratitude and joy.

3 The nativity

Consider the scene in the stable on that first Christmas: Mary with the Child wrapped in swaddling clothes, Joseph watching over them with love and care, the shepherds coming when they hear the angel's message. Ask for the grace to welcome Jesus, however he wants to come to you.

4 The presentation in the temple

Consider Mary and Joseph taking the Child Jesus to the temple to offer him to the Father, and Simeon's prophecy that a sword would pierce Mary's heart. Ask for the grace to bear suffering willingly for Jesus' sake and for parents to love their children even when they are a cause of pain.

5 The finding of the Child Jesus in the temple

Consider Jesus at twelve years old when his parents search for him in Jerusalem at Passover time and find him after three days. Ask for the grace to be sensitive to the needs of growing children as they find their independence, and for perseverance in seeking Jesus in your own life.

The Sorrowful Mysteries

1 The agony in the garden

Consider Jesus in the Garden of Olives, praying that his Father will spare him the passion if it is possible. His disciples sleep, and so Jesus faces his agony alone as he accepts the Father's will and goes forward to suffer on our behalf. Ask for the grace to seek and accept God's will even when it is costly.

2 The scourging at the pillar

Consider Jesus cruelly whipped by men who show no mercy. He has consented to undergo his passion out of love for us and to bear pain patiently. Ask for the grace to suffer sickness or pain when it comes, and pray for all who at this moment are undergoing torture or are in any way helpless before their tormentors.

3 The crowning with thorns

Consider Jesus mocked as a king, his head running with blood, exposed to crowds who clamour for his death. Ask for the grace to think well of others even when they cause us suffering, and pray for all who are mocked because of some disability or handicap.

4 The carrying of the cross

Consider Jesus weighed down under the cross as he bears it to Calvary. Ask for the grace to carry your own cross in union with him, and in a spirit of solidarity with all who are suffering in mind or body.

5 The crucifixion

 Consider Jesus dying in agony on behalf of the human race, showing us what it really means to continue loving and forgiving to the last. Ask for the grace to love and forgive others as Jesus has done; and pray for all who will die today, for the grace of a happy death for them, and for yourself when the time comes.

The Glorious Mysteries

1 The resurrection

Consider Jesus rising in glory on Easter morning and the joy of his mother and the disciples as they realize that he has conquered death for ever. Ask for the grace of a deep faith in the risen Lord, and pray for those who mourn the loss of a loved one, that they may be comforted.

2 The ascension

 Consider Mary and the disciples seeing Jesus ascend to his Father and knowing that they will see him no more on earth. Ask for the grace to believe in the continued presence of Jesus with us through his Church, and pray for those who seek him in hidden ways, finding it difficult to believe he is with them in darkness.

3 The descent of the Holy Spirit

Consider Mary and the disciples receiving the Holy Spirit while at prayer in Jerusalem. Ask for the grace to be filled with the Spirit of courage and joy to proclaim Jesus to the world, and pray that others may recognize his presence in your life and in the lives of all Christians.

4 The Assumption

Consider the happiness of Mary as, after her death, she joins her Son, body and soul in the glory of heaven. Ask for the grace to reverence your own body and the bodies of others, destined as we all are for glory, and pray for those who abuse or are abused by  others, that they may realize that our bodies are the temples of the Holy Spirit.

5 The coronation of Our Lady in heaven

Consider Mary received by Jesus into his presence and rewarded for her life of faithfulness. Ask for the grace of final perseverance, and pray for all friends, family and dear ones, that we may all meet one day in heaven and praise God for ever.

The Mysteries of Light

Recently Pope John Paul II added five new mysteries called the Mysteries of Light, dealing with the public life of Jesus. These are: the baptism of Jesus, the wedding at Cana, the preaching of the kingdom, the Transfiguration, and the gift of the Eucharist

1 The baptism of Jesus in the Jordan

Consider Jesus at the start of his ministry being baptized by John in the River Jordan. He hears the voice of the Father proclaim him as the Beloved Son, and is filled with the Spirit ready for his mission. Ask for the grace to live out your own baptism more faithfully as a beloved son or daughter of the Father.

2 The wedding at Cana

Consider Jesus going to the wedding with his disciples and changing water into wine so that all the guests might have a good time and the newly-weds not be embarrassed. Ask God to bless all married couples with joy in each other, and for those marriages that are struggling ask for the grace of a new beginning and a new joy born from the waters of suffering.

3 The preaching of the kingdom

Consider Jesus travelling around proclaiming the good news of the kingdom. For us he is ready to endure weariness, contradiction and misunderstanding as he strives to make known the love of the Father. Ask for blessings upon all who strive to spread the gospel, and ask that you too may become a witness by your own manner of life.

4 The Transfiguration

Consider Jesus shining like the sun between Moses and Elijah. Jesus sums up in himself both the Law and the Prophets of the Hebrew Scriptures. Peter, James and John see his glory and know that Jesus is the Messiah, the Promised One of God. Ask for

the grace to know Jesus better and to reflect his brightness
for others.

5 *The gift of the Eucharist*

Consider Jesus offering his Body and Blood at
the Last Supper under the form of bread and
wine. He is ready and willing to leave us the
greatest proof of his love as he goes forward
to his passion and death. Ask for the grace to
receive Jesus more worthily in this sacrament,
and be ready, as he was, to lay down your life
for others.

Selection of hymns

O esca viatorum

O food of travellers, angels' bread,
Manna wherewith the blest are fed,
Come nigh, and with thy sweetness fill
The hungry hearts that seek thee still.

O fount of love, O well unpriced,
Outpouring from the heart of Christ,
Give us to drink of very thee,
And all we pray shall answered be.

And bring us to that time and place
When this thy dear and veiled face
Blissful and glorious shall be seen –
Ah Jesu! – with no veil between.

Pange, lingua, gloriosi

Of the glorious body telling,
O my tongue, its mysteries sing,
And the blood, all price excelling,
Which the world's eternal king,
In a noble womb once dwelling,
Shed for this world's ransoming.

Given for us, for us descending,
Of a virgin to proceed.
Man with man in converse blending,
Scattered he the gospel seed,
Till his sojourn drew to ending,
Which he closed in wondrous deed.

At the last great supper lying
Circled by his brethren band,
Meekly with the law complying,
First he finished its command.
Then, immortal food supplying,
Gave himself with his own hand.

Word made flesh, by word he maketh
Very bread his flesh to be;
Man in wine Christ's blood partaketh:
And if senses fail to see,
Faith alone the true heart waketh
To behold the mystery.

Therefore we, before him bending,
This great sacrament revere;
Types and shadows have their ending,
For the newer rite is here;
Faith, our outward sense befriending,
Makes the inward vision clear.

Glory let us give, and blessing
To the Father, and the Son;
Honour, might, and praise addressing,
While eternal ages run;
Ever too his love confessing,
Who, from both, with both is one.

Jesus, my Lord, my God, my all

Jesus, my Lord, my God, my all,
How can I love thee as I ought?
And how revere this wondrous gift,
So far surpassing hope or thought?
  Sweet Sacrament, we thee adore,
  O make us love thee more and more.

Had I but Mary's sinless heart
To love thee with, my dearest King,
O with what bursts of fervent praise
Thy goodness, Jesus, would I sing.
  Sweet Sacrament, etc.

Ah see, within a creature's hand
The vast Creator deigns to be,
Reposing, infant-like, as though
On Joseph's arm, or Mary's knee.
  Sweet Sacrament, etc.

Thy Body, Soul and Godhead, all,
O mystery of Love Divine,
I cannot compass all I have,
For all thou hast and art are mine.
  Sweet Sacrament, etc.

Sound, sound his praises higher still,
And come, ye angels, to our aid,
'Tis God, 'tis God, the very God,
Whose power both man and angels made.
  Sweet Sacrament, etc.

O Jesus Christ, remember

O Jesus Christ, remember,
When thou shalt come again,
Upon the clouds of heaven,
With all thy shining train –
When every eye shall see thee
In deity revealed,
Who now upon this altar
In silence art concealed.

Remember then, O Saviour,
I supplicate of thee,
That here I bowed before thee
Upon my bended knee;
That here I owned thy presence,
And did not thee deny,
And glorified thy greatness
Though hid from human eye.

Accept, divine Redeemer,
The homage of my praise.
Be thou the light and honour
And glory of my days.
Be thou my consolation
When death is drawing nigh;
Be thou my only treasure
Through all eternity.

O Bread of heaven, beneath this veil

O Bread of heaven, beneath this veil
Thou dost my very God conceal.
My Jesus, dearest Treasure, hail;
I love thee, and adoring kneel.
Each loving soul by thee is fed
    With thine own self in form of bread.

O Food of Life, thou who dost give
The pledge of immortality;
I live, no, 'tis not I that live,
God gives me life, God lives in me.
He feeds my soul, he guides my ways,
    And every grief with joy repays.

O Bond of love, that dost unite
The servant to his living Lord;
Could I dare live, and not requite
Such love – then death were meet reward:
I cannot live unless to prove
    Some love for such unmeasured love.

Beloved Lord, in heaven above,
Where, Jesus thou awaitest me;
To gaze on thee with changeless love;
Yes, thus I hope, thus shall it be:
For how can he deny me heaven
    Who here on earth himself hath given?

Hail, thou Living Bread of heaven

Hail, thou Living Bread of heaven,
Sacrament of awful might:
I adore thee, I adore thee,
Every moment, day and night.

Heart, from Mary's heart created;
Heart of Jesus, all divine,
Here before thee I adore thee
All my heart and soul are thine.

Soul of my Saviour, sanctify my breast

Soul of my Saviour, sanctify my breast;
Body of Christ, be thou my saving Guest;
Blood of my Saviour, bathe me in thy tide;
Wash me, ye waters, gushing from his side.

Strength and protection thy his passion be,
O Blessed Jesus, hear and answer me.
Deep in thy wounds, Lord, hide and shelter me,
So shall I never, never part from Thee.

Guard and defend me from the foe malign.
In death's dread moments make me only thine;
Call me, and bid me come to thee on high,
Where I may praise thee, with thy saints for aye.

O thou, who at thy Eucharist didst pray

O thou, who at thy Eucharist didst pray
That all thy Church might be for ever one,
Grant us at every Eucharist to say,
With longing heart and soul, 'Thy will be done.'
O may we all one bread, one body be,
One through this sacrament of unity.

For all thy Church, O Lord, we intercede;
Make thou our sad divisions soon to cease;
Draw us the nearer each to each, we plead,
By drawing all to thee, O Prince of peace.
Thus may we all one bread, one body be,
One through this sacrament of unity.

We pray thee too for wanderers from thy fold;
O bring them back, good shepherd of the sheep,
Back to the faith which saints believed of old,
Back to the Church which still that faith doth keep.
Soon may we all one bread, one body be,
One through this sacrament of unity.

So, Lord, at length when sacraments shall cease,
May we be one with all thy Church above,
One with thy saints in one unbroken peace,
One with thy saints in one unbounded love:
More blessed still, in peace and love to be
One with the Trinity in unity.

Discendi, amor santo

Come down, O love divine,
Seek thou this soul of mine,
And visit it with thine own ardour glowing.
O comforter, draw near,
Within my heart appear,
And kindle it, thy holy flame bestowing.

O let it freely burn,
Till earthly passions turn
To dust and ashes in its heat consuming;
And let thy glorious light
Shine ever on my sight,
And clothe me round, the while my path illuming.

Let holy charity
Mine outward vesture be,
And lowliness become mine inner clothing.
True lowliness of heart,
Which takes the humbler part,
And o'er its own shortcomings weeps with loathing.

And so the yearning strong,
With which the soul will long,
Shall far outpass the power of human telling;
For none can guess its grace,
Till he become the place
Wherein the Holy Spirit makes his dwelling.

Just for today

Lord, for tomorrow and its needs
    I do not pray,
Keep me, my God, from stain of sin,
    Just for today.

Let me both diligently work,
    And duly pray,
Let me be kind in word and deed,
    Just for today.

Let me be slow to do my will,
    Prompt to obey;
Help me to mortify my flesh,
    Just for today.

Let me no wrong or idle word
    Unthinking say;
Set thou a seal upon my lips,
    Just for today.

Let me in season, Lord, be grave,
    In season gay;
Let me be faithful to thy grace,
    Just for today.

And if today my tide of life
    Should ebb away,
Give me thy sacraments divine,
    Sweet Lord, today.

In thine own dread but cleansing fires
    Brief be my stay;
Oh, bid me, if today I die,
    Go home today.

So, for tomorrow and its needs,
    I do not pray;
But keep me, guide me, love me, Lord,
    Just for today.

Long ago in Nazareth

Long ago in Nazareth dwelt a Virgin fair,
Spring was in her heart and spring was in the air.
All underground the seeds were sprouting green,
Love would bloom with them though now they were unseen.

'Hail O Holy Mary,' spoke an angel voice,
'For the Lord is with you, sing aloud, rejoice!
Laid in dark earth, to mortal eyes unseen
Love will come to you like wheat that springeth green.'

'I am the Lord's servant,' answered she with grace,
And the joy of springtime shone upon her face.
Love in her womb, would blossom where had been
Nothing but the soil for wheat that springeth green.

So the darkened world will radiant be with light,
For an angel's message pierces through life's night.
Love now will live where death and sin have been,
Mary shall bring forth the wheat that springeth green.

Joyfully to Mary Virgin let us sing,
All for she gave us Jesus Christ our King.
Love did she bear, of love is she the Queen,
Love has come to us, like wheat that springeth green.

Thou who didst summon

Thou who didst summon thy servant Richeldis,
Bidding her build to thine honour a Shrine,
Help us to follow in thy blessed footsteps,
Framing our lives on the pattern divine.

Countless the pilgrims whose footsteps have echoed
Down through the years along Walsingham's Way;
Countless the prayers that thy children have offered;
Mary of Walsingham, hear us, we pray.

Many long years saw thine image neglected,
Only a few sought the help of thy prayers:
Walsingham's Shrine now again in its beauty
Welcomes each pilgrim who thither repairs.

Pray for us then, blessed Mary, our Mother,
Pray for thy children who kneel in thy Shrine,
Pray that thy Son upon England thy Dowry
Pour down his favours and blessings divine.

So shall we praise thee with ceaseless thanksgiving,
So shall we sing of thy love and thy power,
So shall we feel thy protection and comfort
All through our lives and in death's solemn hour.

Virgin-born, we bow before thee

Virgin-born, we bow before thee:
Blessed was the womb that bore thee.
　　Mary, Mother meek and mild,
　　Blessed was she in her Child.

Blessed was the breast that fed thee;
Blessed was the hand that led thee;
　　Blessed was the parent's eye
　　That watched thy slumbering infancy.

Blessed she by all creation,
Who brought forth the world's salvation,
　　And blessed they – for ever blest,
　　Who love thee most and serve thee best.

Virgin-born, we bow before thee:
Blessed was the womb that bore thee.
　　Mary, Mother meek and mild,
　　Blessed was she in her Child.

Sing of Mary, pure and lowly

Sing of Mary, pure and lowly,
Virgin-Mother undefiled.
Sing of God's own Son most holy,
Who became her little child.
Fairest child of fairest Mother,
God the Lord who came to earth,
Word made Flesh, our very Brother,
Takes our nature by his birth.

Sing of Jesus, Son of Mary,
In the home at Nazareth,
Toil and labour cannot weary
Love enduring unto death.
Constant was the love he gave her,
Though he went forth from her side,
Forth to preach, and heal, and suffer,
Till on Calvary he died.

Sing of Mary, sing of Jesus,
Holy Mother's holier Son.
From his throne in heaven he sees us,
Thither calls us every one.
There he welcomes home his Mother
To a place at his right hand,
There his faithful servants gather,
There the crownèd victors stand.

Joyful Mother, full of gladness,
In thine arms thy Lord was borne,
Mournful Mother, full of sadness,
All thy heart with pain was torn.
Glorious Mother, now rewarded
With a crown at Jesus' hand,
Age to age thy name recorded
Shall be blest in every land.

Hail, Queen of Heav'n, the ocean Star

Hail, Queen of Heav'n, the ocean Star,
Guide of the wanderer here below,
Thrown on life's surge, we claim thy care,
Save us from peril and from woe.
Mother of Christ, Star of the sea,
Pray for the wanderer, pray for me.

O gentle, chaste, and spotless Maid,
We sinners make our prayers through thee,
Remind thy Son that he has paid
The price of our iniquity.
Virgin most pure, Star of the sea,
Pray for the sinner, pray for me.

Sojourners in this vale of tears,
To thee, blest advocate, we cry;
Pity our sorrows, calm our fears,
And soothe with hope our misery.
Refuge in grief, Star of the sea,
Pray for the mourner, pray for me.

And while to him who reigns above,
In Godhead one, in Persons three
The Source of life, of grace, of love,
Homage we pay on bended knee,
Do thou, bright Queen, Star of the sea,
Pray for thy children, pray for me.

In splendour arrayed

In splendour arrayed,
In vesture of gold,
The Mother of God
In glory behold!
O daughter of David,
Thou dwellest on high,
Excelling in brightness
The hosts of the sky.

O Maiden thou art
A Mother renowned;
A mother who yet
As virgin art crowned;
The Lord of the angels,
God high and supreme,
Took flesh of thy substance,
The world to redeem.

All kindreds and tongues
Thine offspring adore,
Creation must bow
His footstool before;
At thy gentle pleadings
May he from his height
Disperse all our shadows
And fill us with light.

The Father we praise,
Who chose for his Son
A Mother all-pure,
Th' immaculate one.
All praise to her offspring
Who saveth our race:
Alike to the Spirit,
Who filled her with grace.

Mary immaculate, star of the morning

Mary immaculate, star of the morning,
Chosen before the creation began,
Chosen to bring, for thy bridal adorning,
Woe to the serpent and rescue to man.

Here, in an orbit of shadow and sadness
Veiling thy splendour, thy course thou hast run;
Now thou art throned in all glory and gladness,
Crowned by the hand of thy Saviour and Son.

Sinners, we worship thy sinless perfection;
Fallen and weak, for thy pity we plead;
Grant us the shield of thy sovereign protection,
Measure thine aid by the depth of our need.

Frail is our nature, and strict our probation,
Watchful the foe that would lure us to wrong.
Succour our souls in the hour of temptation,
Mary immaculate, tender and strong.

See how the wiles of the serpent assail us,
See how we waver and flinch in the fight;
Let thine immaculate merit avail us,
Make of our weakness a proof of thy might.

Bend from thy throne at the voice of our crying,
Bend to this earth which thy footsteps have trod;
Stretch out thine arms to us living and dying,
Mary immaculate, Mother of God.